Tiger Slayer

Tiger Slayer

The Extraordinary Story of Nur Jahan, Empress of India

Ruby Lal

Illustrated by
Molly Crabapple

NORTON YOUNG READERS
An Imprint of W. W. Norton & Company
Independent Publishers Since 1923

For all the young adults of our world

Copyright © 2025 by Ruby Lal and Molly Crabapple

All rights reserved
Printed in South Korea
First Edition

For information about permission to reproduce selections from this book, write to
Permissions, W. W. Norton & Company, Inc., 500 Fifth Avenue, New York, NY 10110

For information about special discounts for bulk purchases, please contact
W. W. Norton Special Sales at specialsales@wwnorton.com or 800-233-4830

Manufacturing by Prinpia
Book design by Hana Anouk Nakamura
Production manager: Delaney Adams

ISBN 978-1-324-03033-1

W. W. Norton & Company, Inc., 500 Fifth Avenue, New York, NY 10110
www.wwnorton.com

W. W. Norton & Company Ltd., 15 Carlisle Street, London W1D 3BS

1 2 3 4 5 6 7 8 9 0

Contents

Introduction: *Story Makers* vii
Major Characters xiii
The Mughal Empire Under Akbar, 1605 xiv

One: *Miracle Girl Born on the Road* 1
Two: *Caravan Nursery and Beyond* 12
Three: *The Mirror of Happiness* 19
Four: *When Mihr Became Nur* 36
Five: *Light of the Palace to Light of the World* 48
Six: *Nur Becomes Co-Sovereign* 65
Seven: *Portrait for an Empress* 74
Eight: *Delayed Honeymoon* 83
Nine: *Baby Taj* 95
Ten: *Anarchy* 107
Eleven: *A Daring Raid* 118
Twelve: *The Long Journey* 136

Acknowledgments 153
Sources and Notes 157
Index 163

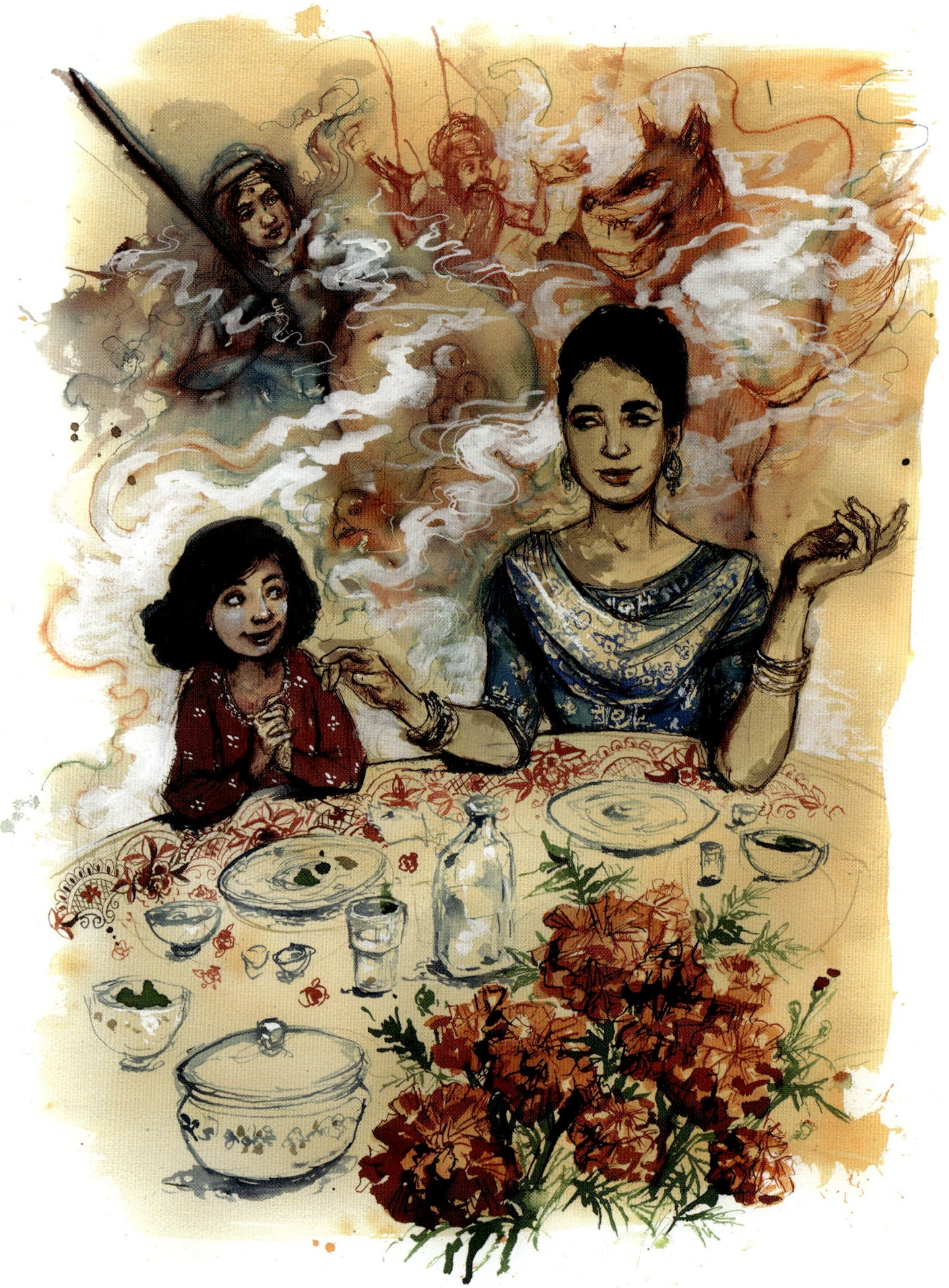

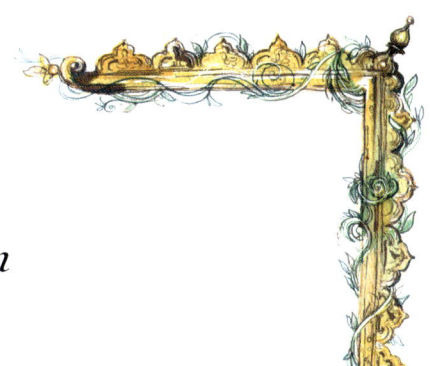

Introduction

STORY MAKERS

Some time ago there was a thin and restless girl growing up in India. She lived with her parents and two younger sisters in a beautiful valley called Dehradun. Full of groves of luscious lychee trees, and famous for its sweet-smelling long rice, her hometown was tucked at the bottom of the Himalayan mountains. Each day when she came home from school for lunch, she would run up to the rooftop with her younger sister. The dense green hills were not that far out. They would stand, stare at the hills, and swiftly run downstairs when called to table.

Soon her father, a civil engineer, would come home. A kind man with sea-green eyes that blended with his brown skin, he took care of the little girls. He served them meals, asked about school, and was—mostly—merry at the table.

It was quite an effort to make this girl eat. She liked only rice and lentils. She made a sad face, hands cupping her cheeks, if her favorites were not on the menu. But even as she made faces, her little black eyes furrowed in the absence of rice and *daal*; she also ate up her vegetables and drank a big glass of buttermilk. Because if she didn't, there would be no afternoon story.

Mom was the storyteller. With high cheekbones and sharp eyes, Mother was a loving but exacting woman. Father was lenient: when his daughters complained of a mild tummy ache, which they did every now and then, he would argue with Mom and let them have a day off. But Mother allowed no excuses. It was never easy to get a day off from school.

The girl didn't complain of stomach aches too often. She enjoyed history classes, for she loved stories. She saw the world in stories. And she relished her mother's tales. A parrot advising its owner. A clever fox fooling some peasants. The valor of the queen of Jhansi, who fought against British rule in India. Legends of Victoria, the British queen. And India's *Romeo and Juliet, Heer-Ranjha*. On weekends, her father listened from the sidelines, hidden behind his newspaper.

One hot summer afternoon, the girl waited eagerly for her mother to finish her chores, put the baby to sleep, and get to story time. Her sister was busy eating oranges. At long last, the girl and her mother sat on the floor and began playing *gaind-gitta*, a game like the American game of jacks. You bounce a small ball with one hand. Make a cave shape with the palm of the other hand. The cave-shaped palm rests on the floor. You slip one of your five dice at a time into the cave as the ball dances up.

That day, the girl was bored with the game. "I want a story," she said to her mother.

Nearly four hundred years ago, a great empress lived and ruled in India, Mother began. *Her name was Nur Jahan.*

The girl's mother said the empress was a *Queen of Queens*.

She didn't come from a royal family, but she ruled the empire. She was strong and just. She wrote beautiful poetry. She designed gorgeous wedding dresses of red and gold. She built gardens full of mango and tamarind trees. She seized a gun and saved her people from killer tigers.

The girl was in a trance. Her eyes lit up. Nur felt more real to her than other heroines her mother spoke about. She was not from the royal family. She was born on the road. She slayed tigers.

INTRODUCTION

The gun-wielding poet-empress of India had conquered the girl's imagination.

Another girl with long black hair and the prettiest little nose was growing up in New York, in a part of the city then full of wild dogs that stalked the streets. Her mother was an illustrator for toy companies and children's books. The girl loved to be in her mother's studio, adoring the Greek gods, princesses, and the Cabbage Patch Kids that came out of her mother's brushes and pens. She saw the world as art. Art was everywhere. Tall and short trees, folds of people's dresses, high-heeled shoes that she wanted but couldn't buy—she didn't have the money.

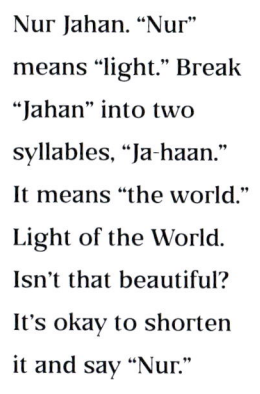

Nur Jahan. "Nur" means "light." Break "Jahan" into two syllables, "Ja-haan." It means "the world." Light of the World. Isn't that beautiful? It's okay to shorten it and say "Nur."

She was an avid reader. Books kept her company. But she didn't like her school. Her teachers found her reading art books and stories, not paying attention to the classwork.

When she became a teenager, she often hung around the Metropolitan Museum of Art. There, she was besotted by miniature paintings from India.

Miniature, yes: it means extremely small. This was how many court painters drew: seated on the floor, one leg bent, holding delicate rice paper. Minute images on a page the size of your hand. And yet, you can see every detail: the feather of a bird, the eyes of the dancers, the folds of their clothes, guns, cannons, forts, mosques, elephants, horses, kings, queens, boys and girls, hunting, and battles. And the colors! Rose pink, ink blue, mud yellow, sunny gold. Each page is decked with a gold border. Inside the rim, twisting and winding green creepers and lilies and magnolias.

The girl spent a lot of time in the museum, in libraries, looking at books in secondhand shops, wherever she could. One day, she found a book with mesmerizing pictures of the poems of a famous Persian poet by a French artist, Edmund Dulac.

The poems that Dulac drew his scenes for were written nine hundred years earlier. They were world-famous. Want to know the name? *Rubaiyat*. Four lines in each poem, a compact style. What were the poems about? A bearded wise man teaching his students; cozy wooden wine inns where brilliant men and women gathered; saints and sages discussing the problems of the world. The pictures had tulips and cypresses and angels and sultans.

No wonder the girl was taken by Dulac's lively illustrations of these ancient poems. Women in long flowing skirts with little flowers, transparent veils thrown casually over their heads. Shinning black eyes. Red leather books. Dazzling peacocks. An old man rubbing his white beard as he lounged. She recognized the blue-and-white leaves, the soft texture of the folds of dresses, people moving in paintings. They had the same dazzle as that of the Mughal miniatures she had seen at the museum. When she saw the pictures Dulac drew, the girl sensed the power she could have as a painter.

Now that you know the story maker and the artist of this book, let's begin Nur's history. Let's go back in time, to 1577, more than four hundred years ago. It was a very, very different world. Back then, whether they were kings and queens or ordinary citizens, people traveled in large groups. Riding upon camels and horses, sometimes in caravans of thousands of men, women, and children. Whole cities. Quite often, they went thousands of miles across deserts, rivers, and mountains. In one of these caravans Nur's parents traveled from Persia to India. Our empress was born on the way.

Major Characters

Mihr un Nisa (later named Nur Mahal and Nur Jahan)

Ghiyas Beg, Mihr's father
Asmat Begum, Mihr's mother
Dai Dilaram, midwife, nurse, later head of the imperial harem
Asaf, Mihr's brother (one of her five siblings)

Ali Quli Beg, Mihr's first husband
Ladli, daughter of Mihr and Quli; married Jahangir's son Shahryar

Akbar, the third Mughal emperor
Harkha, wife of Akbar, mother of Jahangir

Salim (later named Jahangir), Akbar's son, succeeded Akbar as emperor; Mihr's second husband

Khusraw, eldest son of Jahangir
Khurram (later named Shah Jahan), second son of Jahangir; the favorite and the presumed heir; married Arjumand, daughter of Asaf and thus Mihr's niece
Parvez, third son of Jahangir
Shahryar, youngest son of Jahangir

Dawar Bakhsh, Khusraw's son, Jahangir's grandson

Mahabat Khan, a military officer

Herat

Persia

Kandahar

Kabul

Srinagar

Kashmir

Punjab

Lahore

Indus River

Delhi

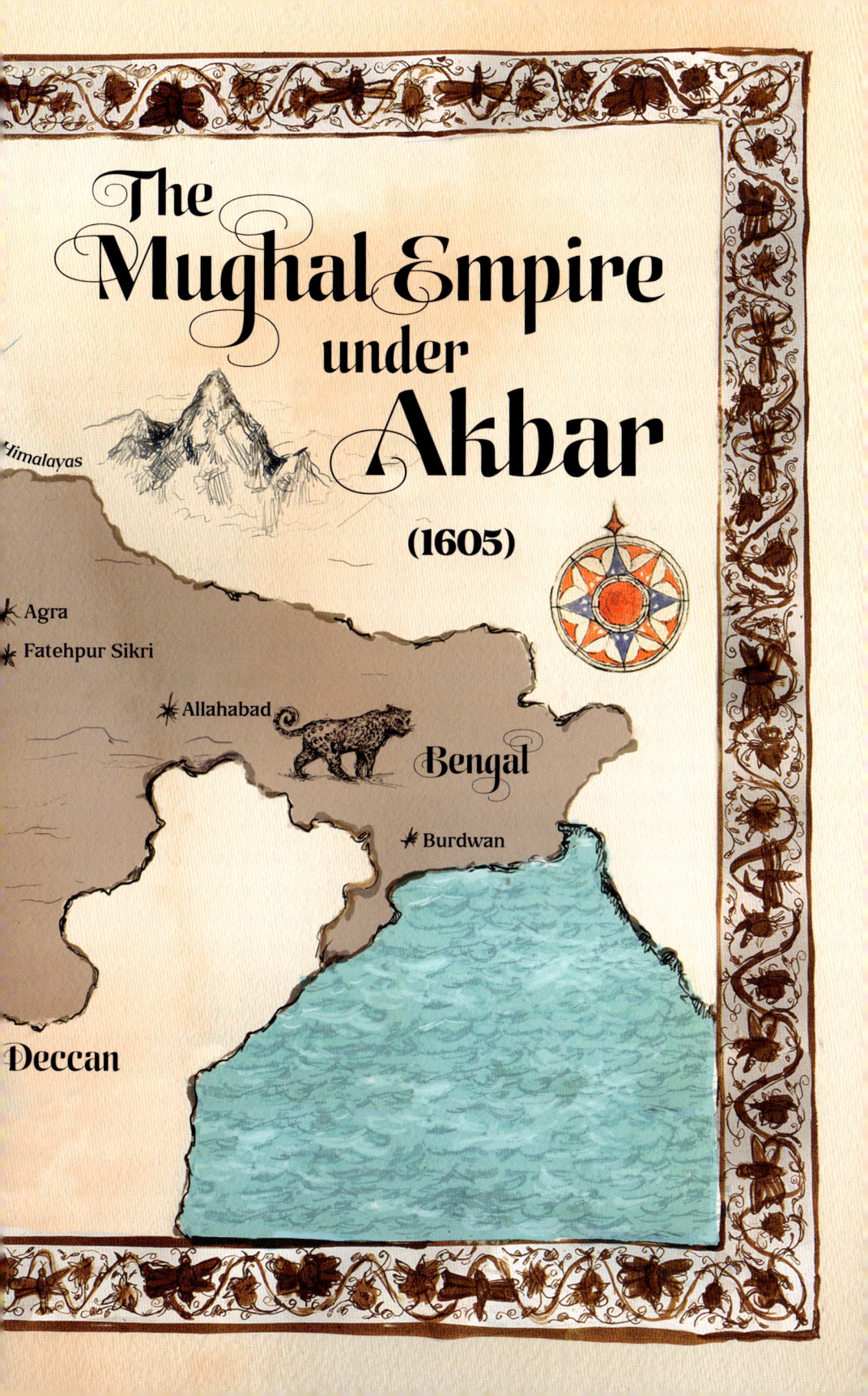

The Mughal Empire under Akbar
(1605)

Himalayas

Agra
Fatehpur Sikri

Allahabad

Bengal

Burdwan

Deccan

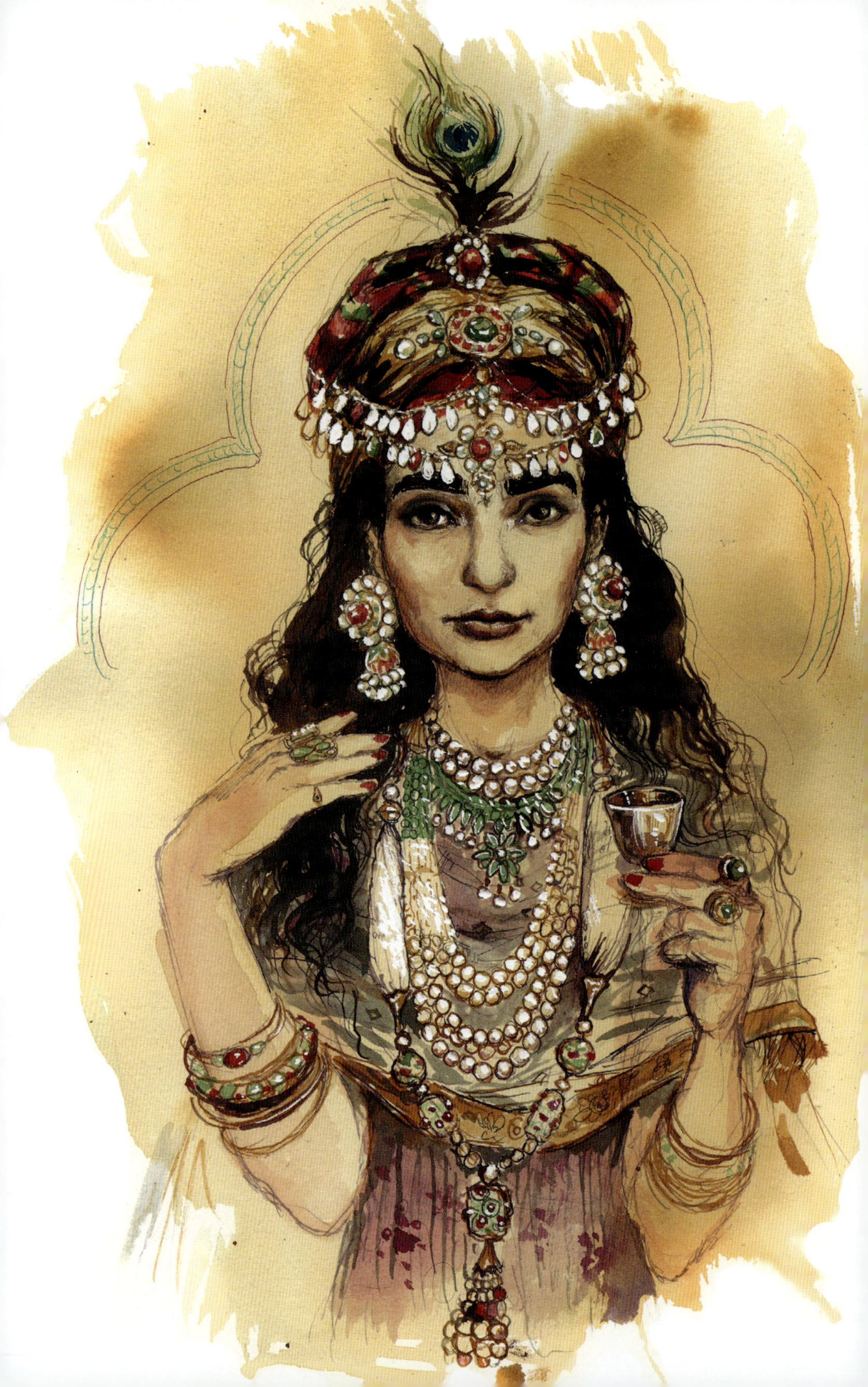

Tiger Slayer

One

MIRACLE GIRL BORN ON THE ROAD

In the autumn and winter of 1577, a large comet passed startlingly close to Earth. People could see it clearly in the sky. European astronomers called it the Great Comet. In India, the Mughal emperor Akbar was spellbound. He invited his astrologers to give their opinion on the comet's shape and effects.

Ancient astrology books described more than a hundred kinds of comets. Some had tails, others forelocks. They heralded both good and bad fortune. The Great Comet was twin-tailed and intensely bright. It was blinding to look at. It could be seen in most of Europe and over India, Tibet, parts of China, Central Asia—and Persia.

The royal astrologer said to Emperor Akbar that troubles would come to Persia, in particular. He was right. Visitors soon reported that the Persian king had died and his kingdom was suffering from economic afflictions and bloody political upheaval. What no one knew was that the season of the comet had brought another historic event. On the road outside Kandahar, in what is now Afghanistan, a girl was born. Her parents were leaving Persia for India, or Al-Hind, as Persians called it then, meaning "Across the river Hind." In those days, people recognized places by rivers and mountains.

> The Mughals were the royal family that ruled India for more than three hundred years, starting in the early 1500s. They were Muslim rulers. Nur, the empress in our story, was married to the fourth Mughal emperor.

Ghiyas Beg, the girl's father, was a trim man of twenty-two with gentle brown eyes. He was intelligent and open-minded, an expert in calligraphy, writing beautiful curved script. Asmat Begum, her mother, was a good-looking woman, learned and lively. The couple came from noble families. We can say that they were like many other liberal members of the ruling class. Men of the Persian upper class drank wine, recited poetry, and talked politics. Women were accomplished in the arts of writing, horseback riding, and politics. They shared poetry with one another. They shopped for clothing and lace in the marketplace and visited the *hammam*, the bathhouse, where

> Persia is the old name for Iran. Pronounced: "E-raan." Not "ran" but "raan." It is a country in the continent of Asia. Nur's parents went to India from Persia. So, Nur was Persian.

they laughed together, shared secrets, and spoke frankly about sex. Men and women discussed epics, fables, poetry, accounts of travel, stories of land rivalry and battles among the rulers. Although theirs was a gender-divided society in which men and women spent a lot of time apart, the sexes mixed at family dinners, picnics, and musical gatherings.

> Beg and Begum: these are titles of honor, like "Lord" and "Lady," that tell us that these people were from an elite background.

Why did the couple leave? Like India, Persia at that time was a land with a tolerant culture. People of many backgrounds and religions lived together: Persians, Armenians, Arabs, Jews, Christians, Muslims of many sects, mystics. The ruling royal family respected all kinds of faiths. But it was also a place where such broadmindedness went in and out of fashion.

Mystery surrounds the exact troubles Ghiyas faced. In 1577, both the tolerant Persian king and Ghiyas's father died. Ghiyas was in the service of the king as a revenue officer in one of the districts of Persia. He was in debt, and now his father was no longer alive to help him. The new king was less relaxed about any kind of opposition, liberal views, even music. Ghiyas was a liberal man. He might reasonably have thought his life was in danger, debt or no debt.

So, along with Asmat, he decided to leave his homeland in search of a better future. For several decades, Persian artisans, soldiers, religious leaders, physicians, calligraphers, musicians, dramatists, and dignitaries had gone to the wealthier, more tolerant Mughal India. *The abode of peace, a place of refuge*: that is how people described the court of Akbar. An uncle of Asmat's was already there. A military general, he fought a major war on behalf of the emperor.

Persia covered what is today's Iran, northwest Afghanistan, and parts of countries like Georgia and Armenia. Due to the hilly and arid topography, the agricultural produce in Persia was low, but it was well known for its silk. Its population: ten million.

Mughal India covered today's north and central India, Pakistan, Bangladesh, and part of Afghanistan. Mughal India was one of the world's wealthiest states, with huge agricultural production and nearly one hundred million people, a population matched only by China's.

The Great Comet was glowing overhead. Asmat and Ghiyas left their home in Herat, called the pearl of the region of Khorasan. A vibrant city, Herat sat at the intersection of major trade routes that ran from the Mediterranean to both India and China, and was well known for its textiles, bathhouses, and gardens. A wall with four large gates surrounded the city. The family exited through the Kandahar Gate, which meant that they were headed toward the city of Kandahar, 350 miles southeast. They had with them their two sons and a daughter. Asmat was once more pregnant.

Those were the days when you could not get from one part of the world to another in a matter of a day or two. It took months. In sixteenth-century Asia, large groups of people moved in long processions or caravans. Royal or elite groups or ordinary people: everyone went in caravans. A king's caravan stretched over several miles and included family members, courtiers, soldiers, and servants. Camels, horses, and elephants by the hundreds carried tents and provisions for huge camps.

Traders transported their goods by caravan. Sometimes passengers joined such commercial caravans. That's what Ghiyas, Asmat, their children, and their servants did. A merchant named Malik Masud led the caravan. Horses, mules, and camels carried saddlebags. Carts were packed with merchandise. Tents, supplies, and grain for the animals were also brought along. The travelers replenished their store of water along the way.

Masud followed a stretch of the Silk Road, the well-known ancient network of trade routes linking East and West. After leaving Herat, they went south through low hills and gently sloping valleys with springs and rivers. They crossed vineyards and cotton fields. There were also melon and apple farms and orchards in the early part of their journey.

Anyone who saw Ghiyas, Asmat, and their children on the road would know they were of noble background. Their clothing was elegant. He wore a flowing cloak and an elaborate turban, and she, a delicate long robe over trousers, her head and upper body wrapped in a velvety shawl. Attendants by their side indicated their high status. A midwife was with them. Her name was Dai Dilaram.

"Dai": midwife or a person trained to assist in childbirth.
"Dilaram": "raam," with a long "a."

Caravan travelers decided their halting points by how far a camel could go in a day. At the time Ghiyas and Asmat went through these parts, there weren't many roadside inns. Most often travelers pitched their tents near water, under the shade of trees, or in roadside orchards, depending on the season.

Travelers ate garlic, onions, and dried apricots, and fed them to their animals. Sometimes burdened horses and mules suffered so much that they collapsed. Caravans traveled with spare camels and horses without loads to replace them.

Close to the Helmand River, north of Kandahar, was a beautifully wooded but dangerous area. Thieves often attacked and robbed caravans there. Bandits armed with swords wounded and even murdered travelers.

Just before Masud's caravan crossed the river, brigands attacked. Asmat and Ghiyas lost a lot of their belongings. Some records say that they lost everything except a couple of mules. Did the caravan guards fight the thieves? Did anyone die in the skirmish? We don't know.

Soon afterward, Asmat went into labor. The midwife and a small band of servants erected a separate tent to ensure privacy for Asmat. Men weren't allowed to view or help with the birth of a child. Asmat gave birth to her baby, a girl. The Great Comet of 1577 was still glowing in the sky. The baby arrived before the turn of the year, a Sagittarius or Capricorn. People in those days believed that comets, eclipses, and arrangements of the zodiac shaped an individual's disposition and attitudes.

After the baby's birth, the midwife cleaned and wrapped her in a white cloth, as prescribed in the family's religion, Islam. Ghiyas offered prayers of thanks for the safe arrival of his new daughter. She was a beautiful infant. She surely brought a moment of pleasure to the caravan amid the hardships of the road. The couple named their daughter Mihr un Nisa, or Sun of Women. We'll call her Mihr.

This migrant girl born on the road would later become the empress of Mughal India.

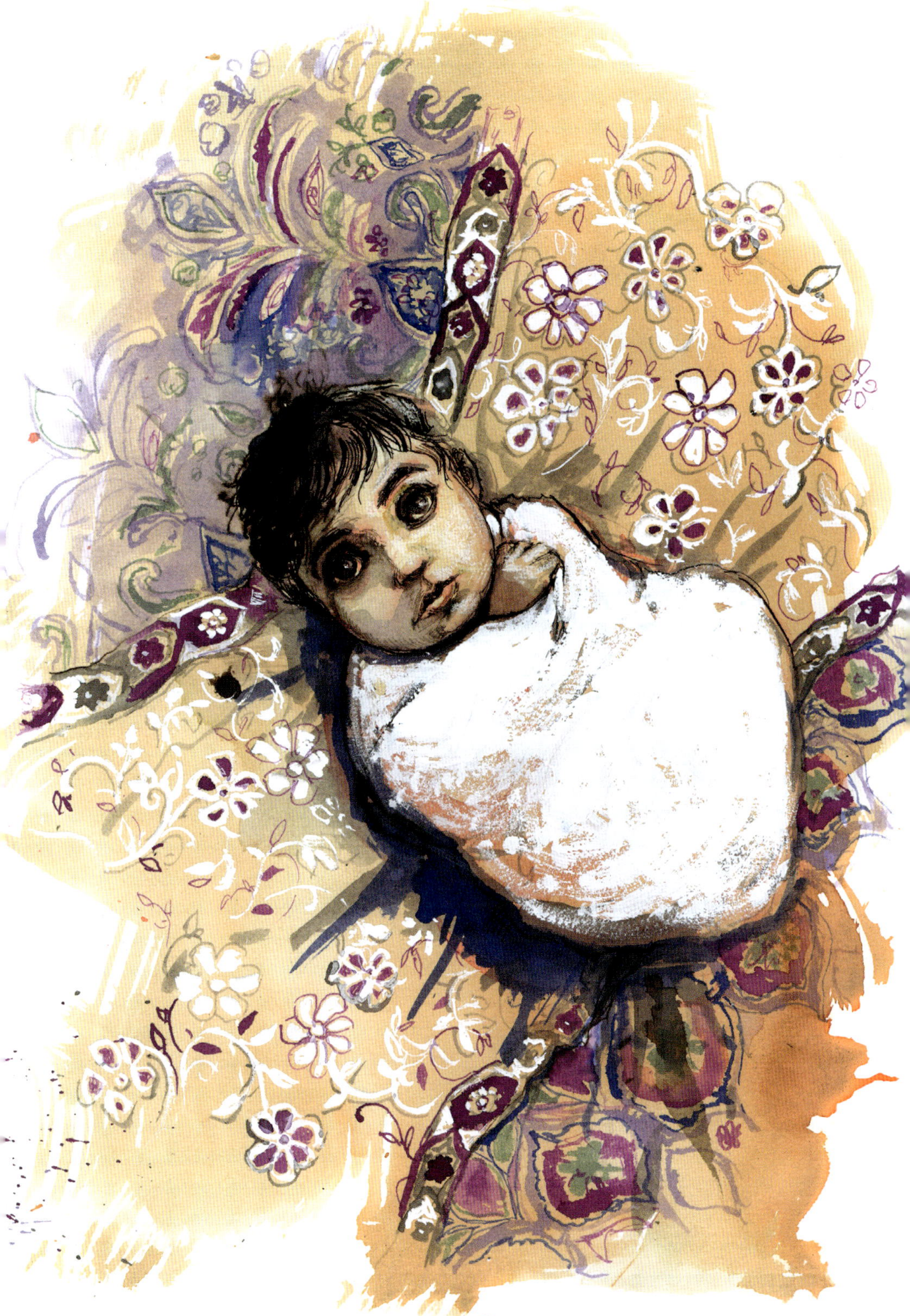

On Sources and Legends

Historians write history with the help of what we call "sources." A source can be many things: the annals of an empire that a king commands someone to write, a diary, or a biography. For example, Nur's second husband, Emperor Jahangir, wrote a memoir: the *Jahangirnama*, or *The History of Jahangir*. There was a poet who wrote about the daring actions of Nur. These are sources. Later you'll read about a portrait of Nur holding a musket. You'll also see the tomb she designed for her parents. Poetry, architecture, coins, and pictures are also sources.

Then there are legends. A bit like stories, legends are created by people when they are allured by a figure, such as Mihr, who later became an empress. Legends can be based on gossip, or they can be pure fantasy. But they hold some truth. They are magical and they are real.

One legend of Mihr's birth described her father steering a donkey carrying the pregnant Asmat. You may recognize this scene. In the Christian Bible, Joseph guides the Virgin Mary to safety on a donkey. The man responsible for this legend was Niccolao Manucci, an Italian and a devout Catholic, who came to India in 1653 and lived there for sixty years.

In another story, written about 150 years after Mihr's birth, a historian, Khafi Khan, says that Ghiyas and Asmat made a desperate decision when Mihr was born. Fearful that they would not be able to provide for the newborn because they'd been robbed, they abandoned her by the roadside in the dead of night. In the morning, the caravan leader, Masud, wandering up and down, spotted the baby by chance. He picked her up. Then, searching for a nurse in the caravan, he noticed Asmat. Knowingly or unknowingly, he gave the baby back to her mother.

A few decades after Khafi's death, another writer, a Scottish man named Alexander Dow, added an enticing new detail to this story of the abandoned baby: a black snake was about to devour her when she was rescued.

Mihr's abandonment, a snake, her rescue—so many twists and turns.

Even if Mihr was not abandoned, even if there was no snake, people thought her birth was magical. She was a miracle girl born on the road. The difficult condition of her birth, people believed in those days, was a sign of distinction from the cradle. Everything else that later happened was only more and more astonishing.

Two

CARAVAN NURSERY AND BEYOND

A couple of months after Mihr was born outside Kandahar, her family crossed the river Indus into India. Holding on to whatever they were left with, they arrived in the land of the Great Mughal.

For those coming from the northwest, the nearest and first major point of entry to the Mughal lands was the city of Lahore. This was where Ghiyas, Asmat, baby Mihr, and her siblings arrived.

The caravan was Mihr's first nursery. Imagine a baby in a caravan all those months! The city of Lahore was her second nursery, totally different. It had bustling bazaars and delightful gardens, and a mix of languages and cultures. It was a grand and prosperous place that sat in the rich farming region of Punjab.

In most Indian towns and cities of that time, nobles and

> "Punjab" is made of two words. "Punj" means "five," and "ab" means "water"—literally, the land of five rivers. And the rivers spread like the five fingers of a hand.

landlords opened their homes to visiting relatives and friends, and also to travelers, merchants, workers, servants, and the poor. The owner's family usually kept a substantial part of their residence for private use but gave part over to visitors. It was in the culture to be welcoming to people from other parts of the world, and people were keen to hear stories of far-off lands. Some lodgers stayed for free, some paid rent, and some worked for their room and board.

The caravan leader, Masud, introduced Ghiyas and Asmat to a Persian man in Lahore. He helped them find a place near the fort. That would be their home until they began the final leg of their journey to the Mughal emperor's court in the city of Fatehpur-Sikri, 350 miles to the southeast.

The area was pulsating with energy. Merchants selling everything from horses to silk thread to muskmelons congregated outside the fort. Streets were crowded with houses, and bazaars packed with buyers, sellers, and passersby exchanging greetings and news. One section of the bazaar, a maze of narrow lanes, was set aside for women only. They took their time gazing at the bold patterns and colorful embroidery on muslins, silks, and velvets. Many wore flowers in their hair, as well as toe rings and anklets with charms or little bells, and chewed betel leaf to redden their lips.

The aromas of cooked food mixed with whiffs of raw meat from the stalls. Persians loved rice. Here it was served in piquant dishes such as *biryani*—rice with meat, onions, peppers, cinnamon, cumin, and other spices. There was also rice and meat cooked in a gravy or broth with onions. There were breads large and small, baked in the oven or made in skillets. Lots of fruit, yogurt, ghee (clarified butter), aromatic spices—and sugary sweets.

What languages did the travelers hear? Hindavi, from which modern Hindi was born. And Punjabi, among many other languages. Their melodious mother tongue, too. Many Persian speakers, including scholars, poets, and administrators, had settled in Lahore. Booksellers in the markets of Lahore and other Indian cities, such as Delhi and Agra, sold books of Persian poetry. The fourteenth-century Persian poet Hafiz had said that Persian was so irresistible that someday "all the Indian parrots [poets]" would relish "this Persian candy." Persian candy!

There was fantastic music. In homes and inns, sublime poetry full of mentions of wisdom and wine and love was recited aloud. Mihr's parents would have felt at home among all this. But they stayed in Lahore for only a few months. It was a stopover so that the family could rest and adjust to a new environment—including the grand Indian elephants, green parrots, and bright blue peacocks. Ghiyas had time to think his way forward, and consider the best possible plans. Remember that Asmat's uncle was employed by the Mughal emperor, Akbar. This was a good connection. The uncle had already found a place for a cousin in the court. Now it would be Ghiyas's turn.

Between the end of 1578 and early 1579, the family reached Fatehpur-Sikri, the Mughal capital—the Red City.

Its grand new buildings were made of red sandstone from the nearby quarries. Gardens were cooled by the leafy shade of mango and neem trees and lush henna bushes. Studded with domes and cupolas, the tiled rooftops of the palace could be seen as soon as visitors entered the city gates. They could also see the massive mosque. Near the palace was a tower decorated with sculpted elephant tusks, to show that the brave, energetic, and fierce emperor captured and dominated elephants. In the open space outside the palace, Akbar and his court enjoyed polo, elephant fights, gladiatorial battles, and acrobatics. Below the palace were the travelers' lodgings where Ghiyas and Asmat and the children first stayed.

The emperor's name—Akbar—literally means "great." He was world-famous as *Grao Mogor*, *Groote Mogul*, and *Grand Mogol*, as the Portuguese, Dutch, and French called him. Akbar gave two audiences every day. At sunrise, kettledrums rang. After Akbar had finished his morning rituals and prayers, he would come out on one of the balconies of the palace. Showing himself like a god, he blessed his people from on high.

The Beautiful Story of Fatehpur-Sikri

Emperor Akbar was in despair. Although he'd had several children from his many marriages, all of them had died. Wise men suggested that he seek the blessings of a Sufi holy man named Salim Chishti, who lived in the village of Sikri. (The Sufis were mystics in Islam, known to be liberal-minded, and lovers of poetry and music).

Clad in a knee-length gold-embroidered silk cloak, Akbar sat beside the saint. Salim blessed him and foretold that he would have three sons.

When his eldest son was born, Akbar built Fatehpur-Sikri to honor the saint. He named his son Salim, after the Sufi. "Fatehpur" means "City of Victory." Sikri was the village of the saint.

But Mihr's father met Akbar in a second, private audience for nobles, officers, ambassadors, and traders from other parts of the world. Such meetings took place in the State Hall toward the close of the day or sometimes at night. There the emperor announced court appointments.

The spacious State Hall was located at the eastern end of the palace. Tucked into one side of the State Hall was a pillared courtyard. There Akbar sat cross-legged on an elevated rug-draped red sandstone throne. He wore a knee-length gold-embroidered silk cloak that was tied at the waist with an embroidered belt. The imperial dagger hung at his side. He wore a lambswool shawl, tasteful necklaces of gold and pearls, finger rings, and gold-embroidered shoes with pointed toes.

A large drum began to beat. Bodyguards, princes, grand nobles, and men who, like Ghiyas Beg, had permission to attend stood barefoot in their designated places. Akbar's oldest son, Prince Salim, then age ten, was always near him. The second and third princes stood farther away. Railings of gold separated the emperor from nobles of the highest rank. Then a silver railing, behind which stood another group of nobles of lesser rank. Beyond a wooden railing were the rest of the men in the hall. There were no women.

The master of ceremonies, the courtier in charge of protocol, called out Ghiyas Beg's name. Dressed in a flowing orange cloak and an elaborate turban, tasteful attire in the presence of the emperor, he stepped forward. He would have been told in advance not to wear red or yellow; those colors were reserved exclusively for Akbar. Ghiyas placed the palm of his right hand upon his forehead and bent his head forward. In this pose, he performed the obligatory *kornish*—a sign of submission to the royal presence.

Silence was an important part of court etiquette. Those admitted to the emperor's presence weren't supposed to start a conversation. Ghiyas stood before the Grand Mughal in stillness. If the emperor turned to look at a courtier or raised an eyebrow toward him, that courtier would be pleased. If the emperor spoke, he would feel blessed.

The emperor took the measure of Ghiyas Beg, who stood humbly, head slightly bowed, hands folded. The emperor must have been pleased. Following the audience, Ghiyas Beg was given employment in the imperial government. His first job and starting rank are not known, but he would rise fast, to great heights.

As he left his first audience with Akbar, Ghiyas offered the emperor *taslim*, a salutation in which he placed the back of his right hand on the ground, then raised it gently until he stood erect, putting the palm of his hand upon the crown of his head. After repeating this three times, Ghiyas set forth on his new Indian career.

With employment secured, Ghiyas and his family could settle in Fatehpur-Sikri. A large house in the center of the city became Mihr's first home.

Three

THE MIRROR OF HAPPINESS

At the edge of the world, in a sea where fish danced, lay the legendary island of Wak-Wak. On it stood a talking tree, with heads of humans and demons growing from its branches amid leaves and flowers. Heads of beasts sprouted from its roots: lions, tigers, dragons, elephants, and *simurghs*, mythical flying creatures. It was said that Alexander the Great visited the talking tree of Wak-Wak.

The story of the Wak-Wak tree is certainly among those Mihr heard as she grew up in her Sikri mansion. Others would have come from *Tales of the Parrot*, in which a wise parrot told enticing stories each night to distract his mistress from having an affair while her husband was away on business. Her mother might have told her that the parrot was like Scheherazade, from *The Thousand and One Nights*, known in their family's home in Persia. Her parents would also tell parables from *The Rose Garden* by Sadi, the Shakespeare of Persian literature, stories of the miraculous Baka flower, which cured many diseases, and anecdotes of the awe-inspiring queens and princesses.

Mihr's father's mansion was on the half-mile-long main street of Sikri. It was one of the four major lanes that jutted out in different directions from the central market. A large gate opened into a courtyard, which led into a front yard and a row of rooms. This was the area for men to mingle, conduct business, and meet people. In those days, noblemen and noblewomen spent much of their time in separate parts of the home. This was a typical arrangement in elite homes. Mihr, her mother, and her sisters could not enter the men's area. Female servants were also barred.

Behind the front row of rooms was the women's section. Private rooms were on the upper floor, and shared areas, the kitchen, and the toilet facilities were below. To one side of the courtyard were storerooms, stables, and servants' quarters, with back doors opening onto the street. No men could enter the women's area except Mihr's father and brothers or the older male servants of the house.

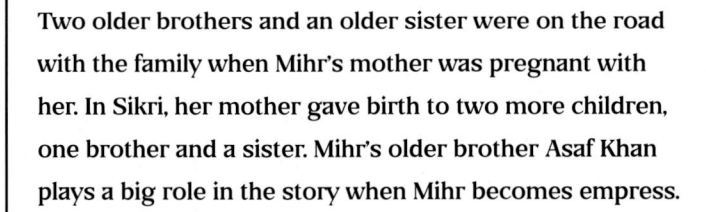

> **Two older brothers and an older sister were on the road with the family when Mihr's mother was pregnant with her. In Sikri, her mother gave birth to two more children, one brother and a sister. Mihr's older brother Asaf Khan plays a big role in the story when Mihr becomes empress.**

Five times a day, Mihr and her siblings would hear the exalting sound of the call to prayer from the mosque. There was also the hammering of workmen's tools, the grunts of cattle and goats, and the conversations of passersby: shoppers going to the Chahar suq, the market, and merchants selling fireworks, fish, wood, soap, and building materials.

In the women's part of the mansion, Mihr wrote the first letter of the Persian alphabet, *alif*, which literally means "commencement" or "inauguration." Writing the first letter was a ceremonial event. It launched learning for boys and girls. Mihr would also learn Hindavi, slowly saying the name of a vegetable or a constellation, the word for summer dust storms, or *Ram Ram*, a common greeting invoking Rama, the popular Hindu deity.

Festivals, ceremonies, and rituals taught the boys and girls to be cultured. They earned spiritual merit by giving clothes, cash, and food to

alif

the needy, ensuring that the poorest were able to rejoice. Being generous was very important.

"Hindavi," from the river Hind, a precursor of the modern Hindi language of India.

As the children grew older, the boys were offered opportunities not given to the girls. There were no formal schools, but royal and aristocratic boys in Mughal India had tutors. Family members, mainly the women of a household, took the initiative in teaching girls. A female teacher, a *muallima*, might be allowed in the elite premises to teach the girls. Sometimes fathers or grandfathers taught them arithmetic or the art of writing. Ghiyas, a master calligrapher, would have demonstrated the beauty of good penmanship to his sons and his daughters.

Parents in those days could be harsh, especially if they read any of the dogmatic guidebooks for raising children that were popular at the time. The author of one famous manual, which Emperor Akbar had read out aloud to him, said girls should be invisible. *They should not be allowed to read or write.*

It is clear that Asmat and Ghiyas were not among the sternest of parents. Even so, they would insist that their children learn to be patient and courteous. Seriousness and daring were believed to look good on a man. Intelligence, tenderness, and self-control were crucial as girls came of age. Indelicate language was not allowed. Archery, swordsmanship, hunting, and managing elephants and horses were for boys. Princesses and aristocratic girls like Mihr learned to shoot and ride horses.

Later in life, Mihr would write sophisticated poetry that showed she was not only highly literate but well read in Persian literature. As empress, she would often seek counsel from her father on matters of governance, which suggests a long-standing close relationship between them. A lover of poetry himself, Ghiyas would introduce her to Iranian masters such as the wise poet Hafiz and the Anatolian mystic Rumi.

Ghiyas and Asmat would see early signs of Mihr's agile mind, her ingenuity, and her literary imagination. She would continue the family's love for poetry and creative thinking that her parents and so many other Persian migrants longed to nurture.

When Mihr was about eight years old, the family moved to Agra, twenty miles away. Emperor Akbar had ordered everyone to leave Sikri because of a water shortage. And since Ghiyas was a member of the court, he would move to Agra. If the emperor moved, so did everyone attached to the court.

Life in their new home would be similar to life in Sikri. Dilaram, the midwife who had helped with Mihr's birth on the road, still served the family, now as head of staff. She cared for the children, helped in the kitchen, and reminded the servants to dust the carpets, light torches in the evening, and fill pots with water to cool the quarters during the blistering summers. She would feed the pet parrot and keep rosewater ready so that guests could cool their hands and faces with a refreshing splash. When a servant arrived from the men's area with a request for a snack or a meal, Dilaram would instruct the cooks to prepare dressed rice, spiced and roast meats, lentils, and bread. She might teach the children chess and Persian backgammon.

Sometimes Mihr and her siblings visited the market or the riverside gardens. But rather than using public streets, elite girls and women traveled over the rooftops, passing from one home to another. They were not supposed to mingle or be seen on the streets.

As Mihr and her sisters were growing up, they enjoyed many

kinds of festivals. Muslims celebrated the great feast of Eid at the end of a month-long fast. At the court the emperor gave a feast. Archers shot from horseback. Courtiers played polo. Mihr's father and brothers would delight the girls with descriptions of these court events. They also celebrated the Night of Salvation: a night full of promising that they would not sin—no lying or cheating or being unkind or violent.

In autumn, Hindus performed their glorious epics in theater. The *Ramayana* was a grand story about good and evil. Mihr would hear these wonderful stories of Lord Rama and his wife, Sita, from her father. They were a favorite of the Mughal emperor Akbar, Ghiyas's master. Court painters drew numerous beautiful paintings of the events of the life of Rama and Sita. The emperor's mother commissioned her own album of exquisite pictures based on the *Ramayana*.

A Brief Summary of the Ramayana

Rama, prince of the ancient city of Ayodhya, won the hand of the beautiful princess Sita but, through the plotting of his stepmother, was exiled with her and his brother for fourteen years. In the forest Sita was abducted by Ravana, the king of Lanka, and Rama gathered an army of monkeys and bears to search for her. The allies attacked Lanka, killed Ravana, and rescued Sita. In order to prove her chastity, Sita had to walk through fire but was vindicated by the gods and restored to her husband. After the couple's triumphant return to Ayodhya, Rama's rule inaugurated a golden age.

As they grew older, Mihr and her male siblings became more separate from each other. Her brothers would accompany their father to soak themselves in the practices and the atmosphere of the court. Since they had been trained by this time as expert marksmen and learned young aristocrats, the best career possibility for them would be to become well-placed courtiers. Mihr's brothers, among them, the eldest, Asaf—quiet, observant, and determined—would meet the tolerant Emperor Akbar and Prince Salim, the presumed heir to the throne. Salim would be their prime model. It was typical for elite boys to look up to the prince.

Mihr's life was centered in her father's mansion. But legends say that she visited the Mughal palace with her mother. It was not unusual for aristocratic women like Asmat to visit the palace quarters. Legends also note that Salim pursued Mihr during these visits. Once, he caught hold of her hands to express his love. Salim was bewitched by Mihr, they say.

It's certainly possible that Mihr met Salim. It was also said that the emperor instructed Ghiyas to marry off his daughter immediately and recommended a bridegroom. Whether it was because of the emperor's command, we do not know, but in 1594, when Mihr was seventeen, her parents chose a Mughal officer as a groom for her.

> In Mihr's time, parents selected brides and grooms for their sons and daughters.

The mansion was garlanded with flowers, lace, tinsel, strings of bells, and colorful embroidered fringes. The trees in the courtyard were hung with garlands of marigolds and jasmine.

Carved in graceful floral patterns, a wooden and glass screen separated the men's section of the wedding room from the women's. Asmat, Dai Dilaram, and a host of other women surrounded the new bride. Dark-eyed and slender, wearing a fine knee-length silk shirt and long breeches, Mihr sat next to the women of her family. Her clothes were in a deep, dark rose color; heavy brocade decorated the sleeves and hem of the shirt. Seamstresses would make sure that Mihr's wedding shirt was sewn without any knots; they were inauspicious and would fetter fortune. She wore jeweled earrings, rubies. Her shimmering veil of transparent silk, embroidered with gold filaments, was draped loosely over her head, showing her exquisite face.

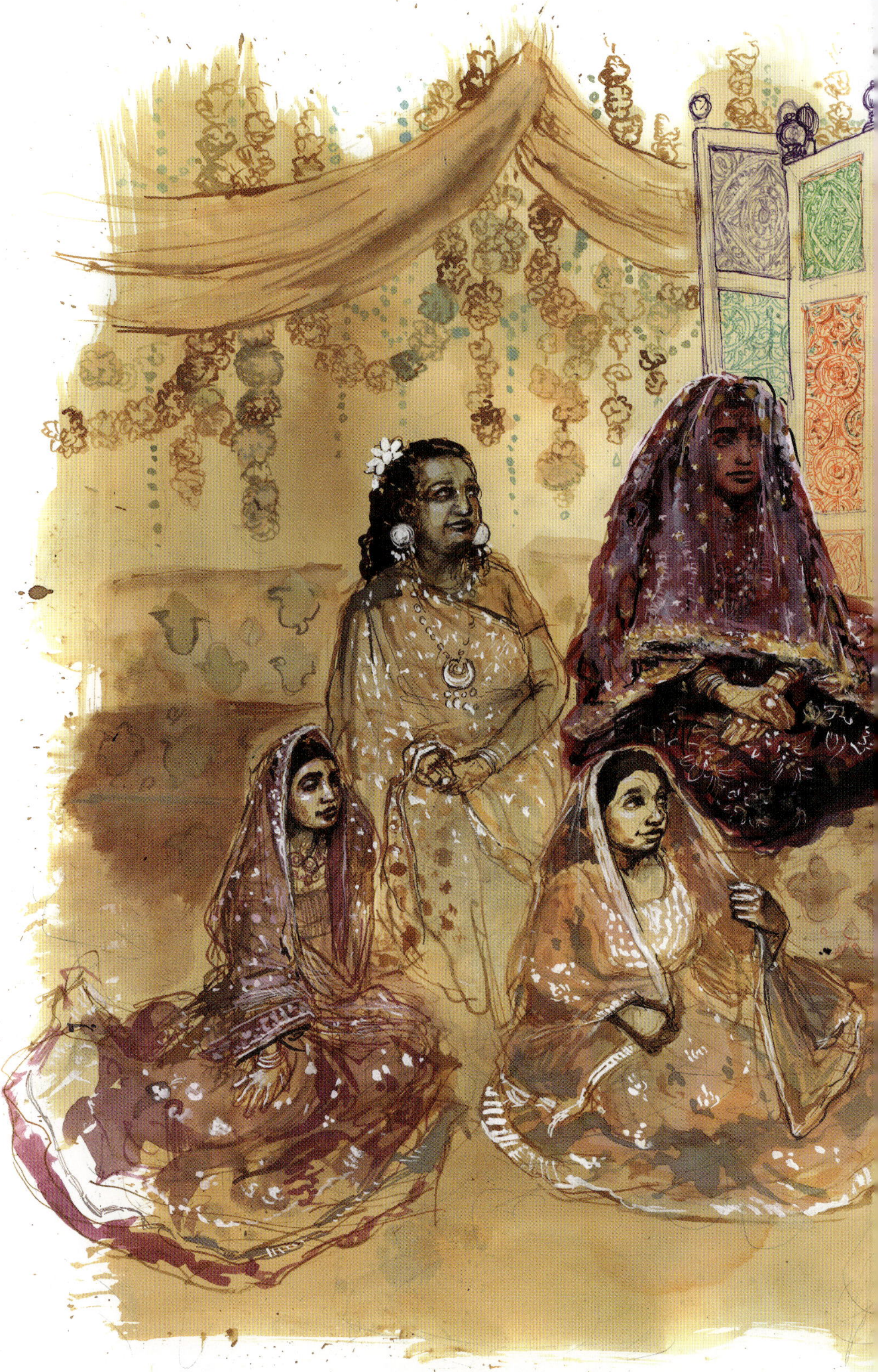

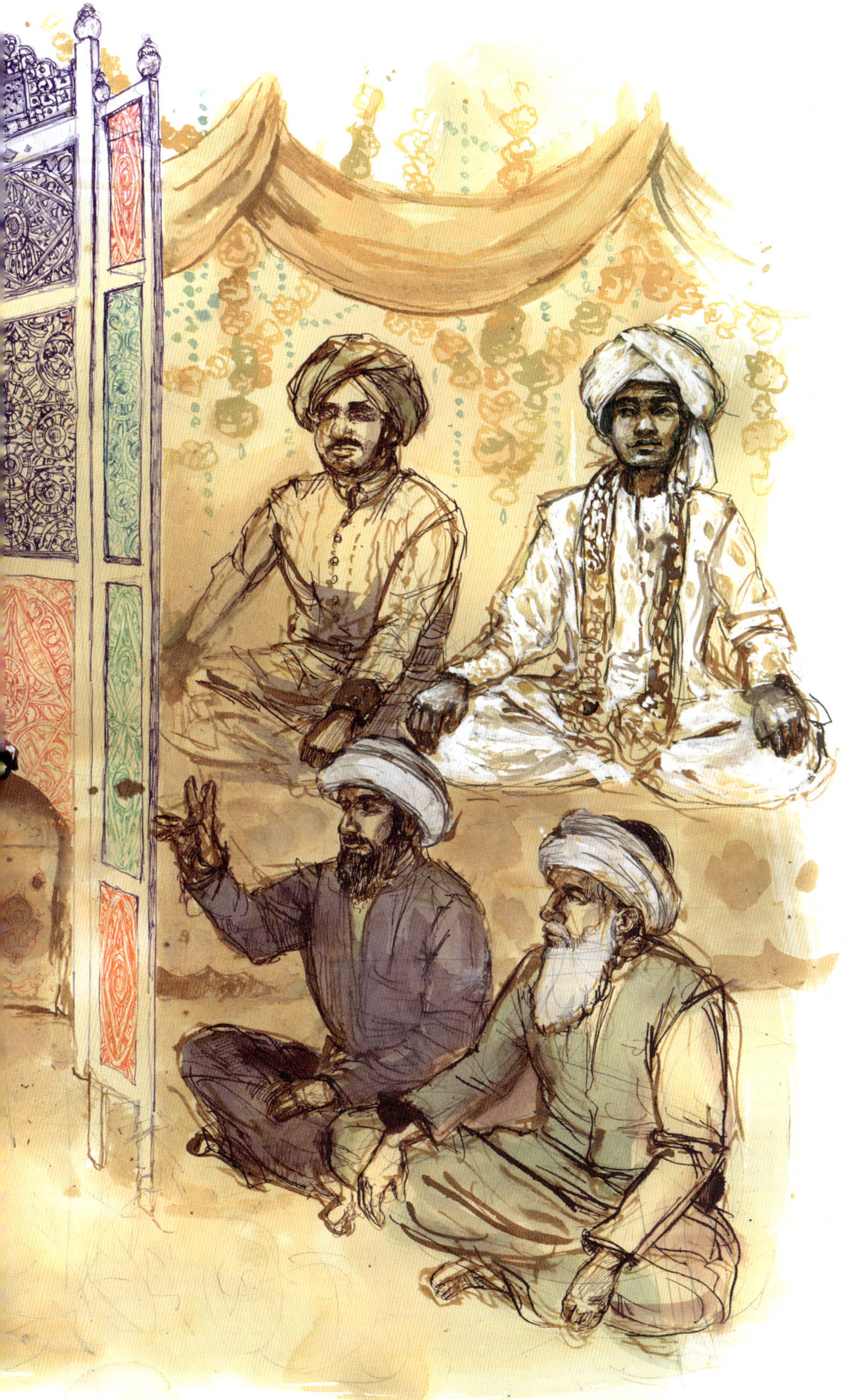

On the other side of the screen—with Mihr's father, brothers, and the other men—was the groom. His name was Ali Quli Beg. Strong and handsome, he wore a graceful silken top and trousers embroidered in gold.

What do we know about Quli? Before coming to India, he was a table attendant of the king of Persia. Like Mihr's parents, he'd left his homeland after the demise of the Persian king.

> In the world of kings and queens, a table attendant was an important officer. A king was always in danger of being poisoned by his enemies, so a table attendant tasted the king's food before serving him. Another important fact: people like Quli were experts at more than one job. Quli was an intimate officer of the Persian king, and a brave warrior.

After leaving Persia, he met a senior Mughal commander about to go into a major battle. Commander Rahim—a poet, translator, and courtier—was one of the finest and most highly regarded nobles of Akbar's court. Quli joined the army and fought bravely. Rahim recommended him for a job in the court. That's how Mihr's father took note of Quli's rising prospects.

The wedding began with a platter sent by Quli to Mihr. It held wild rue, incense, sugar, a small sack of henna, a cake of soap. And a loaf of *sangak* bread—leavened dough made on a bed of stones, inscribed in gold or red with a wish for happiness. Asmat would add a handful of nuts.

The Quran, a prayer rug, the platter, and a mirror called "the mirror of happiness" set the stage for the marriage contract. Two clerics, or mullahs, one representing Quli and the other Mihr, came in and sat in the men's area. Addressing Mihr through the screen, one of the mullahs would ask if she consented to the marriage. After a prescribed modest pause and polite prompting, Mihr would say yes or simply nod her head. The women sitting next to Mihr served as witnesses, confirming her assent. Then the mullah would ask Mihr whether she had received the agreed-upon cash as the marriage settlement. When she said yes, the mullah asked whether she authorized him to marry her to Quli. Once she said yes again, the two mullahs faced each other and pronounced blessings. All the guests would express joy and bless the newlyweds. Women would immediately offer sugared almonds to Mihr, which she would crunch and swallow with her eyes closed. When she opened her eyes, she'd make sure to look upon a little boy among the guests. It was a ritual meant to ensure that her firstborn would be a boy.

Then the screen was taken away. Mihr's mother and sisters would formally introduce her to Quli. He would sit next to her, gazing at her reflection in "the mirror of happiness" rather than looking at her directly. Wild rue burned in a brazier in a corner of the room to ward off evil. The family and guests would shower the couple with sugared almonds and coins. Women would rush forward to retrieve the coins. Quli honored his first direct look at his wife by presenting her with a jewel.

After their marriage, the couple left for a town named Burdwan. Rich with rivers, lush and wild, it was in the province of Bengal to the extreme east of Agra. The loyal servant Dilaram accompanied Mihr. They set off east along the ancient Grand

Trunk Road, a well-traveled route that wound alongside the sinuous Yamuna River. They traveled by covered coaches drawn by oxen, then took boats over the river. It would take them more than a month to reach Bengal. A leading minister of the emperor's court, a man named Raja Man Singh, was the governor. Quli, a junior officer, was accountable to the governor. The governor sent reports to the emperor.

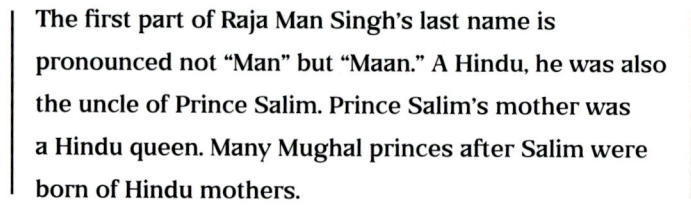

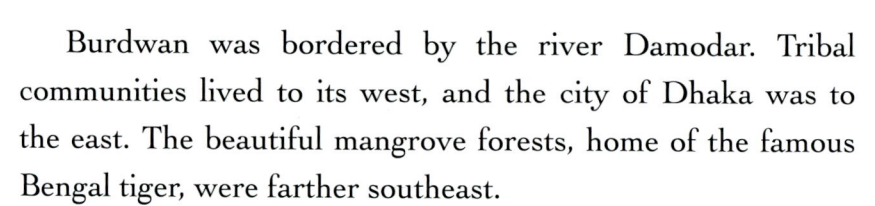

> The first part of Raja Man Singh's last name is pronounced not "Man" but "Maan." A Hindu, he was also the uncle of Prince Salim. Prince Salim's mother was a Hindu queen. Many Mughal princes after Salim were born of Hindu mothers.

Burdwan was bordered by the river Damodar. Tribal communities lived to its west, and the city of Dhaka was to the east. The beautiful mangrove forests, home of the famous Bengal tiger, were farther southeast.

There was a fort, a mosque, and a bazaar in town. And the tomb of a famous saint, a humble water carrier, Sakka, who'd died some thirty years before Mihr's arrival. This is the message she read on his tomb: "The rich should, according to the injunction of the Quran, with pleasure, help orphans, beggars, the afflicted, and the homeless."

For much of the year, people made use of the river and small boats. Come the rains, the embankments would break and floodwaters creep into the mosques, the temples, and the bazaar. Swampy, stagnant pools formed along the river, breeding mosquitoes.

Mihr and Quli's home was to the east of the city, where other officers, revenue collectors, learned men, merchants, and ex-soldiers lived. Houses for the elite were built of bamboo and the wood of the betel-nut tree. Sun-dried bricks were rare. Spacious and beautiful, the houses were flat-roofed. They had gardens with covered walks and outer walls to protect the residents from foxes. Although the dense forests were farther southeast, beasts could creep in.

It was warm through most of the year. No more freezing winters, as in Agra. No more crisp evenings of autumn. In the sultry temperatures and high humidity, Mihr and Quli wore clothes made of cool cotton. Mihr dressed in flowing cotton trousers and blouses, with a light cotton head cover. Quli wore trousers and a knee-length robe that folded around his neck. Compared to Agra, in Bengal people ate more rice—grown in plenty there—as well as fish, herbs, lemons, and vegetables. Green chilies soaked in vinegar was a specialty.

The newlyweds were rather different from each other. Mihr was brainy, an art lover, and a poetry enthusiast. Quli appreciated her curiosity and intelligence. They talked to each other in their common Persian language. She spoke the Hindavi of northern India and would likely have learned Bengali.

Quli was a man of the sword, strong, daring, and dogged. Prince Salim would one day give him the title Slayer of Tigers.

When her husband was away dealing with local landlords or visiting the governor or Agra, Mihr might look at the beautiful landscape and rivers. People in Bengal saw water as a living being. They worshipped the blue god Krishna, the elephant god Ganesha, Saraswati, the goddess of learning, and the goddess Durga, protector from evil.

Mihr would learn about natural cures, trances, the supernatural powers of the goddess Kali. She would hear her assistants in the mansion recite songs as a way of connecting with the gods. This was familiar to her. She had grown up reciting the Quran.

Six years later, around 1600, Mihr gave birth to a daughter. She and Quli named her Ladli, which means "beloved" or "the loved one." Dilaram would be by Mihr's side as she brought her baby daughter into the world.

As a toddler, Ladli would play with stone toys and tortoiseshell and seashell bracelets, and with goats, rams, roosters, and birds such as mynahs and parrots. She might have learned archery or dart throwing or blown toy trumpets.

She would feed on the fresh and fragrant Bengal fish and rice. She would listen to servants, neighbors, and fishermen singing water songs in Bengali, her twin first language along with Hindavi. And the Persian of her parents. A multilingual girl.

The little girl would certainly hear recitals on the *vina*, the stringed instrument of the goddess of learning. She would play in the mansion garden on her own or with the children of the employees, visit the mosque and the bazaar. Or she'd ride with Mihr in a palanquin covered with cloth made from camel or goat hair. There'd be picnics on the river with her parents and attendants. And dice games, polo, elephant fights, and hunting. Ladli would learn rhetoric, logic, and, like her mother, the poetry of the Persian masters. She'd memorize passages from the Quran.

And the legend of the Wak-Wak tree.

Four

WHEN MIHR BECAME NUR

As Mihr went about her life—setting out after game with hunting parties, visiting shrines, nurturing her daughter—she also began to understand how officers ruled in the far-flung areas such as Burdwan. She learned how policies affected poor peasants, women, and children. She heard about the government and the military from her husband.

They would certainly have discussed the death of Emperor Akbar in 1605 and Prince Salim's succession as the fourth Mughal emperor. Upon accession, Salim gave himself a new name: Jahangir.

"Jahan": "the world"; "gir": "to conquer." Thus Jahangir means "Conqueror of the World."

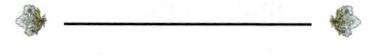

Quli knew that when Jahangir was a prince, he had committed ferocious acts. For example, he put a man to death and jailed two others because they'd accidentally frightened away his quarry while he was hunting. He had a hot disposition. In 1599 he had rebelled against his father and set up a separate court in Allahabad, the famous city on the river Ganges that the Hindus revered. The emperor sent his court loyalist and favored historian, Abul Fazl, to pacify Salim. But the prince had Fazl murdered and sent his head to his father.

Jahangir

> The *Akbarnama*—the name means "*The Book of Akbar*"—is the first history of the Mughal Empire; Emperor Akbar commissioned Abul Fazl to write it. Fazl was celebrated as one of the "nine jewels" of Akbar's court. The Akbarnama is about Akbar's life and times and his dynasty. It includes vivid descriptions of the flora and fauna (the vegetation and animals) of India, as well as the officers, court and harem, and people of those times.

Like many nobles and officers, Quli distanced himself from Salim at the time. He may have been fearful of retribution from

Salim's father, the emperor. Being seen as a supporter of a rebel prince would not bode well for any court officer.

But once Jahangir ascended the throne, he became more humane. He was curious and philosophical. He loved the arts, and invited scholars, poets, and philosophers to court for discussion and debate. He traveled endlessly in majestic cavalcades, taking stock of what was happening in his empire. He built a network of dedicated lieutenants, some from the time when he was a prince and many others from his father's administration. His father had left him a well-established government and a royal treasury worth 150 million rupees in cash. The empire had excellent codes of law, a fine military, and a first-rate administrative, tax, and revenue system. All this built Jahangir's confidence.

> 150 million rupees: equivalent to approximately 1.8 billion in 2025 dollars

But Jahangir did not forget what he saw as Quli's earlier desertion. Quli was wicked and made mischief, Jahangir noted in his memoir. In other histories of that time, we also learn that no sooner did Jahangir become the emperor than his passion for Mihr revived. Whether this is true, we cannot say. What we know is that a drama soon unfolded in Agra that had serious consequences for her life.

This is what happened: Jahangir's eldest son, Khusraw, took up arms against him. Jahangir put Khusraw under house arrest. The prince managed to escape, and fled to the city of Lahore. The emperor appointed men he trusted to secure the Fort of Agra, which housed the royal treasury and the royal women's residences. One trusted adviser was Mihr's father,

Ghiyas, whom Jahangir had honored with the title Confidant of the State. Ghiyas was in charge of Agra while Jahangir went after his rebel son in Lahore.

Officers found the prince and brought him to the emperor with his hands tied, chains fastened from his left hand to his left foot. The prince began to weep, trembling in fear. Jahangir spared his son's life but had his eyes damaged in retribution for his rebellion.

About two years later, Khusraw's supporters plotted to assassinate Jahangir. Mihr's oldest brother, Muhammad Sharif, was part of this conspiracy; he was executed. Her father fell under suspicion and was demoted, fined, and temporarily imprisoned. Hundreds of lower-ranking supporters of the prince were speared or hanged.

Quli was also presumed to be involved in the plot. His lands in Burdwan were confiscated, and Jahangir ordered the governor of Bengal to bring Quli to Agra. The governor went to Burdwan by elephant with a detachment of soldiers on horseback. Quli rode on his horse to greet the dignitary, as would be expected of him. As soon as Quli entered the governor's camp, soldiers surrounded him. Seeing that he was to be taken prisoner, Quli attacked the governor but fell from his horse. The governor's soldiers killed him.

Mihr was now a widow. She mourned for forty days, as was prescribed in Islam. Then an imperial order arrived from Agra, summoning her and her daughter to Agra. When a Mughal officer was killed, his property was forfeited to the emperor—and that included his wife and children.

Dai Dilaram would have accompanied them as they traveled westward on their way to the capital. Twelve years had passed since Mihr had arrived in Bengal. Now her husband was dead; one of her brothers had been executed as a traitor, and her father was under arrest. Her own fate was uncertain.

When Mihr returned to Agra, the capital was even grander and more crowded than when she'd left. Along the banks of the Yamuna River stood many more mansions, surrounded by luxuriant gardens and groves. The Fort of Agra, also on the western bank of the Yamuna, was as imposing as ever. A drawbridge over a moat led to the fort's colossal spiked front entrance gate, decorated with golden loops and rings.

After passing through this door, Mihr and her young daughter would arrive at the front garden of the harem, a multistory palace for royal women. Mihr was sent to the harem rather than to the mansion of her father or older brother because both were under suspicion.

Harem: a royal women's residence, home to generations of women—mothers, wives, and princesses—as well as concubines, foster mothers, and younger princes. A massive wall separated the harem from the public, official quarters where the court business was conducted. Emperor Akbar built the first Mughal walled harem. Before then, although royal women followed codes of modesty, they were not segregated in imperial dwellings. Building a walled harem was part of Akbar's ambition to make his dynasty and his women look awe-inspiring. Inaccessible and unreachable women was the idea. Akbar commanded that women must be "the veiled ones" and live behind harem walls. This was theory. In practice, even from behind the walls, women lived brilliant and daring lives.

There were women guards and officers. Royal eunuchs were stationed at the boundary of the harem precincts, and just outside, male Rajput soldiers guarded the royal dwellings. Aristocratic women like Mihr's mother, Asmat, visited the harem, according to rules put in place by Akbar.

The head officer of the harem would escort Mihr and her daughter to the inner areas. Lavish carvings in floral patterns decorated the walls; vases were carved into niches and etched with leaves and flowers. Blue and red chandeliers hung from the cupola ceilings. Numerous entrances and passages connected a series of open, paved quadrangular courtyards that were lined with trees and pots of plants and flowers and surrounded by verandahs. Behind the verandahs were the royal women's apartments.

Every apartment was spectacularly decorated. There were domes of sandstone, arches so intricately carved that they looked like netting. Although each passage, courtyard, and set of rooms had a distinct style, they were in harmony.

Mihr had visited the harem as a girl. Now she was thirty-one years old. Attractive and dignified, she knew the behavior required of noblewomen connected with the palace, but she had no idea what her role there would be. No longer the head of her own household, she was submerged in a sea of women, in theory, subject to the emperor. Among the hundreds of people living in the harem were the former emperor's elderly wives—that is, Jahangir's mother and stepmothers, Jahangir's nineteen wives, and many concubines.

The emperor's younger sons and daughters, such as three-year-old Prince Shahryar, the youngest, lived in the harem with their mothers. Teenage boys had apartments within the harem. Some moved out when they got married and began their court careers.

Jahangir's second son, Prince Khurram, lived in the harem quarters. Khurram—his name means "joyous"—was the son of a Rajput princess, Man Bai, and Jahangir. When Mihr arrived there, he was sixteen. Mihr's and this prince's futures would be closely tied.

Wet nurses, foster mothers, and their families also dwelled in the harem. There was an immense staff: midwives, scribes, lamplighters, pages, stewards, doorkeepers, oil keepers, cooks, tasters, tailors, palanquin bearers, tanners, water carriers, bookbinders, astrologers, perfumers, weavers, and masons. There were throngs of companions of royal women and their younger offspring. They nursed, bathed, and dressed the

The Four Sons of Jahangir

Khusraw: as we saw, he rebelled against his father.

Khurram, the most beloved son of the emperor and his presumed heir. The Mughals did not follow the rule of primogeniture—that is, the eldest did not automatically succeed as the next ruler. The princes had to show military and networking skills and gather the support of nobles and harem women. Usually, they rebelled against the emperor to prove that they were strong and independent.

The youngest was the good-looking and affable prince **Shahryar**.

Prince **Parvez**: the third son, he drank a lot.

---

children and kept them from harm; they prepared the ladies' baths and filled their smoking pipes, or hookahs.

Mihr would see that Jahangir's wives had restrictions on their lives. They had no control over which of them the emperor visited and when, with whom he had children, to what extent he supported one or another woman—or whom he loved.

Whether Mihr felt stimulated or confined by the social, intellectual, and cultural life of the harem is impossible to say. Nor is it possible to know how harem life affected her daughter, Ladli, who lived sometimes with her mother and sometimes in the mansion of her paternal grandparents. The harem did not allow the individual ambitions of women, certainly not those of innovative younger women. But the harem was a dynamic place. Many women there were lively people with strong interests and desires. Beautiful manuscripts celebrating the empire were housed within the harem; royal women read them and enjoyed the sublime illustrations. Some inscribed their names on manuscripts as signs of ownership. Women wrote poetry and prose.

How Mihr rose from being one among many to become the favored wife of the emperor also remains a mystery. It is possible Jahangir had a long-standing passion for Mihr, as some histories tell us. It's possible that Ghiyas and Jahangir made a marriage arrangement for Mihr: after local rulers or landlords were defeated or fell into disfavor, they often pledged their daughters in marriage to the emperor as a sign of submission. Such an arrangement might explain why three elder harem matriarchs became Mihr's guardians: Salima Begum, whose stepson had once employed Mihr's deceased husband; Jahangir's stepmother, Ruqayya Begum, the oldest matriarch; and his mother, Harkha. These women protected Mihr and guided her on the customs of harem life, such as why giving gifts mattered, when to give gifts and in what order, and the details of Mughal manners and courtesies.

What we know is that on May 11, 1611, when Jahangir was in the sixth year of his rule, he married Mihr. She was described as strong and lovely, and her almond-shaped eyes enhanced her striking look. He was long-limbed, with a muscular but supple body. His skin was neither dark nor fair but somewhere in between; he had dark eyes, curved brows, and an impish smile.

The wedding was a sign of strengthening relations between the emperor and Mihr's family. Prince Khurram was betrothed to Mihr's niece Arjumand, the daughter of Mihr's elder brother Asaf Khan; they married soon after Mihr and Jahangir were married. The year Jahangir married Mihr, he increased her father's rank twice and gave him monetary gifts. The emperor

RUBY LAL

promoted him as *wazir*—minister of the empire, in charge of imperial finance, land assignments, and revenue collection. Mihr's brother Asaf was already a high-ranking court noble. Jahangir now appointed him as imperial steward, in charge of the royal household, treasuries, mints, and construction projects. Her younger brother would get a governorship in the eastern provinces of the empire. The emperor was putting the most important court offices in finance, intelligence, and the military into the hands of Mihr's father and brother Asaf. Many other near and distant family members held appointments in the provinces. Such gathering of power was unlike any the Mughal world had seen.

Everything that followed the royal wedding would confirm that a very special and unusual relationship had begun between Jahangir and Mihr. She would be a sensitive companion and superb caregiver. Soon she would also emerge as an accomplished adviser, hunter, diplomat, and aesthete.

Besotted with his twentieth wife, Jahangir bestowed upon Mihr a new regal name: Nur Mahal, or Light of the Palace. This was the first of what would be her two royal names. Thus, Mihr became Nur.

Five

LIGHT OF THE PALACE
TO LIGHT OF THE WORLD

In the early years of her marriage to Jahangir, Nur's influence in the harem grew. She came to be recognized for her acts of kindness. Her generosity was "boundless and unlimited," wrote Farid Bhakkari, a courtier and author. She bestowed gifts of clothing, jewels, horses, elephants, and cash on royal men and women and gave huge donations to the poor. Frequently she learned through her attendants of destitute girls who wished to wed and organized the marriage and provided a portion of the dowry. She supported the weddings of five hundred orphan girls, and even designed an inexpensive style of wedding dress for brides of poorer families.

Nur's bigheartedness earned her goodwill and admiration from many but, most important, from her new husband. The emperor was so infatuated with the "strength of her personality," said Bhakkari, that the famous lovers Majnun and Khusraw—the Romeos of Islam—paled next to him.

Nur's influence in the harem, with her husband, and, ultimately as empress also grew through her family connections. She became part of an inner circle of influential advisers that included her father, mother, older brother, and her three harem mentors, as well as her lifelong confidante Dai Dilaram. Nur's niece Arjumand and

> Still used today, these types of dresses are referred to as Nur Mahali: in the style of Nur Mahal.

her husband, Prince Khurram, were also part of the powerful royal family group.

In a grand ceremony that took place twice a year in the harem, imperial servants balanced the weight of the emperor on one side of a large scale with an equal weight of articles piled on the other: gold, quicksilver, silk, perfumes, copper, drugs, clarified butter, rice milk, seven kinds of grains, salt, fruits, mustard oil, vegetables. These were later distributed to holy men, and to the poor. Sheep, goats, and fowl in a number equal to the emperor's age were distributed among some lucky farmers. Soon Nur took charge of this semiannual event. "She has considered it a pleasure to do so," wrote the emperor.

A rising force in the harem, Nur was also attuned to the personal needs of the emperor. She eased his concerns about his health, the safety of the empire, and his sons. It may be that other royal wives were as caring and intuitive as Nur, but he hailed her as the one fondest of him. In his memoirs, the emperor described a bout of illness three years into their marriage, when he was "seized with fever and headache."

"I kept this secret from most of those familiar with and near to me, and did not inform the physicians," he wrote. "I only imparted this [the news of his illness] to Nur-Jahan Begam than whom I did not think anyone was fonder of me."

One problem Nur faced was her husband's heavy drinking. He had begun drinking alcohol as an eighteen-year-old during a campaign with his father in the Punjab region. One day while hunting near the Indus River, he felt tired. A gunner suggested that a cup of wine would perk him up. After that, he increased his intake of wine. Then he turned to spirits—such as arrack, a liquor made from fermented rice and date-palm juice. Slowly he moved up to twenty cups, fourteen during the daytime and the remainder at night.

Alcohol and drugs were common in the Mughal world. Wine and poetry went hand in hand during the gatherings of men. Drinking together was a sign and seal of loyalty and royal favor. Nur intervened and tried to help, but the emperor's drinking sometimes impaired his ability to conduct business. Jahangir also used drugs, such as opium.

Along with taking care of her husband, Nur was shrewd about her future. As the most astute and competent of the princes and the favorite of his father, Khurram was the presumptive successor. So, Nur began to support Khurram, perhaps thinking that someday she might continue her influence on government as his wise adviser. Nur feted the prince. And he, knowing of Nur's rising power, extended respect to her in unique ways. On several significant occasions, for example, he offered her lavish gifts. These large cash and other rare gifts were meant to showcase the stature and eminence of the empress.

As Nur closely watched and participated in royal life and its rituals and affairs of state, the Mughal family was closely watching her. She was a new kind of wife with unusual experiences. She had arrived in the harem widowed and already a mother, having looked after an extensive estate in Bengal. She was more canny than other royal women her age, exhibiting the knowledge usually expected of elder women, like her three harem guides.

Many Mughal women had been powerful players, but usually they carried their authority obliquely. For example, they counseled the emperor from their private quarters, intervened behind the scenes to reconcile stubborn princes, and headed important ceremonies.

It was clear that Nur was moving toward a more direct and visible kind of power.

A highly mobile court was the most spectacular feature of Jahangir's reign. That, too, worked in Nur's favor. She traveled the Mughal territories with the emperor and his court. These persistent travels with her husband brought Nur out of confinement. By the end of her life, Nur had traveled the breadth of the empire. It was from a tent that she issued, in the not too distant future, her first imperial order. A legal sign of being a monarch.

When Jahangir married Nur, it was during an unusual period of repose in Agra. Two years after their wedding, he grew restless. He was eager to move about his territories in western India, accompanied by his favorite wife, Nur.

The Peripatetic Court

"Peripatetic" means "traveling from place to place." Babur, the first Mughal king, inherited the tradition of a traveling royal camp from his nomadic ancestors. All Mughal emperors kept up the practice of kingship-on-the-move, even as they settled into grand headquarters in Agra, Lahore, and Fatehpur-Sikri.

They traveled to follow military campaigns, to hunt, and to have the pleasure of novelty. A court on the move was a formidable sign of power. Local landlords and peasants paid their respects to the emperor and were warned of bad behavior.

In the early days of the dynasty, the Mughals' peripatetic culture allowed women greater freedom. This freedom lingered as independence of mind even after Akbar sequestered women in the grand harems of the imperial palaces.

Beginning in early 1613 and continuing for most of the next six years, the Camp of Good Fortune would be home to Jahangir, Nur, her parents, her older brother, and many members of the court as it moved from place to place in western India. The camp was an elaborate portable city and probably held three hundred thousand people: royalty, courtiers, soldiers, and servants.

It stretched for nearly three miles. Canopies embroidered in gold thread shaded the entrances to magnificent trellis tents. There were hundreds and hundreds of them, round, arched, and rectangular. These tents were erected on supple wooden frames covered with waxed cloth, then hung with brocade or velvet. Screens of carved wood and felt pierced in floral patterns separated one section of the camp from another. High red screens clearly marked the harem tents.

A year after the others left Agra, Prince Khurram arrived at the Camp of Good Fortune. The prince was returning from his conquest of the kingdom of Mewar, which was also in western India. In the tented Hall of Special Audience, he greeted his father by touching his feet, a sign of respect. Jahangir welcomed his son and praised him for his victory.

The victorious prince, the emperor, and key courtiers next

went to the red-screened harem. There, Nur was waiting to applaud her stepson. Welcoming him, she presented him with a jeweled sword, a horse and saddle, and an elephant, among other rich gifts. Jahangir had likely discussed with Nur whether to send Khurram to Mewar as commander. The emperor had certainly consulted Nur's father and brother, his chief advisers, about the matter.

Nur knew that Mughals cared deeply about precision in the planning and presenting of gifts. Royal gifts were public declarations of who was backing whom. She'd picked up such subtleties from her experienced father, from her mother, and from the elder Mughal women.

It was Nur and not the prince's mother who received and bestowed gifts on him. In fact, his mother wasn't even part of the royal entourage in the Camp of Good Fortune. Even more

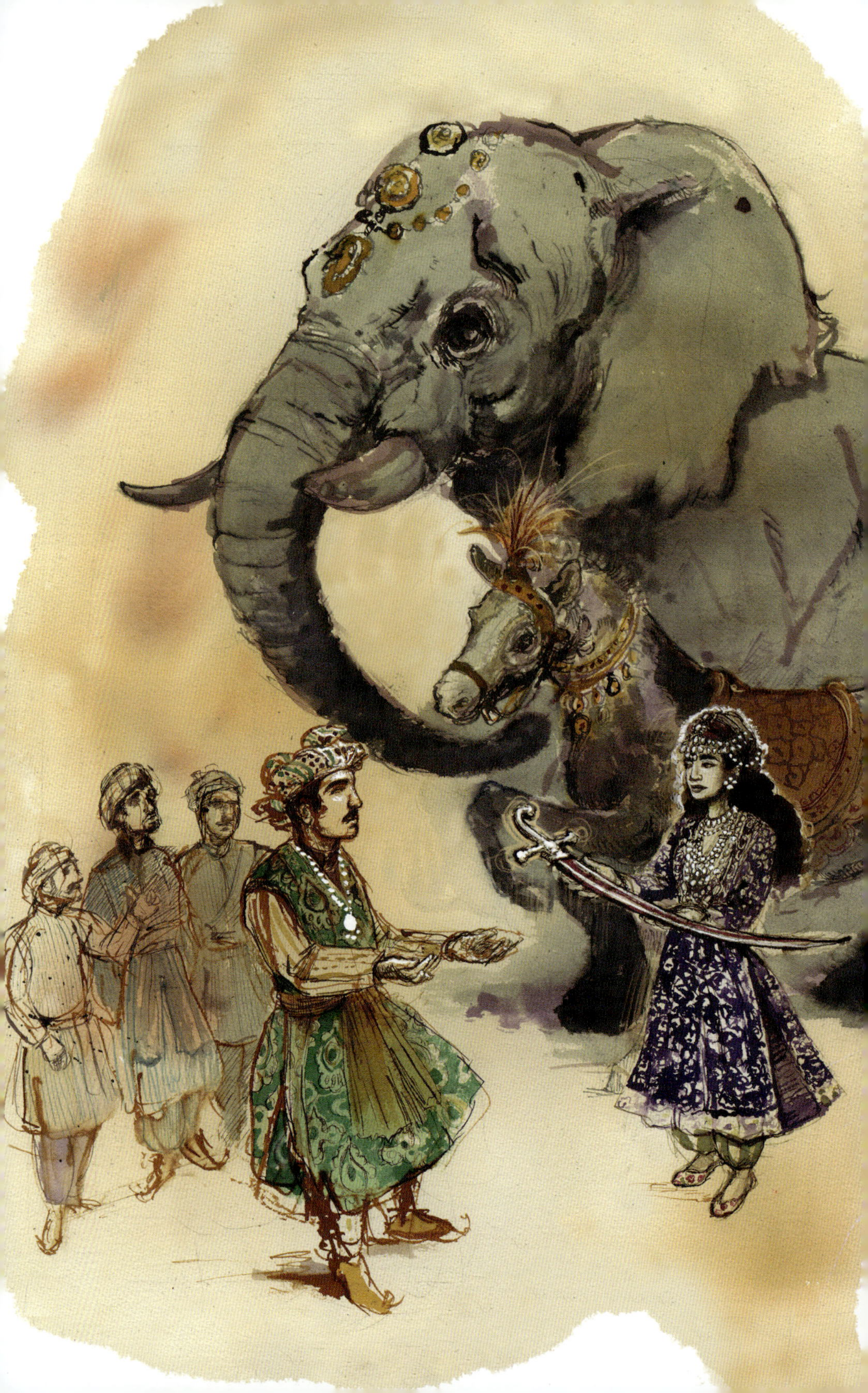

notable is the fact that Khurram paid formal respects to both his father and his stepmother, as if he were reporting to a pair of sovereigns.

From the red-screened section of the camp, a new phase of power had begun for Nur. Three years into marriage with the emperor, she was the most prominent person in the harem.

Feasts, rituals, and official visits continued. One day, Nur's mother, Asmat, was making rosewater. A scum formed on the surface of the dishes into which she poured the hot rosewater. Asmat skimmed off this oily froth and realized that it released a lovely scent. She presented it to her son-in-law, who was much taken by it. "If one drop be rubbed on the palm of the hand," the emperor wrote, "it scents a whole assembly, and it appears as if many red rosebuds had bloomed at once." He presented Asmat with a string of pearls as a reward for her creation.

Maybe this was the scene in Nur's mind when she wrote this poem:

> *If the rosebud is opened by the breeze in the garden*
> *The key to our heart's lock is the beloved's smile*
> *The heart of one held captive by beauty . . .*
> *Knows neither roses, nor color, nor aroma, nor face, nor tresses*

A new campaign plan had been brewing in the Mughal circles. The emperor wanted to expand his territories in the Deccan, the southern Indian plateau to the south of the river Narmada, something even his formidable father had not been able to accomplish. Skilled and brilliant statesmen ruled the south.

Malik Ambar

Especially challenging was Malik Ambar, a slave turned warrior. Born in Ethiopia, Ambar was bought and sold several times by slave dealers during his youth. Fate brought him to India, where he rose to fame as an expert in guerrilla warfare, a seasoned mercenary general, and, eventually, as prime minister in the state of Ahmadnagar.

Prince Khurram was put in command of the campaign, no doubt backed by Nur and her powerful family. Thus, two years after his victory in Mewar, Khurram departed for the Deccan.

The traveling court turned its attention to other activities. Repairs began on two large deteriorating reservoirs and a broken dam. The emperor and Nur made nine visits to the tomb of a revered Sufi saint. They traveled to Pushkar Lake, a sacred Hindu site, fifteen times.

After moving several times, the Camp of Good Fortune came to the town of Ajmer on March 20, 1616. There, a new and unusual honor awaited Nur. After the emperor, Nur, and several royal women paid a visit to her father Ghiyas's tent, Jahangir begged Ghiyas to excuse him. He went back to his tent and issued an edict, a royal decree: "I ordered Nur-mahall Begam to be called Nur-Jahan Begam." The woman known as "Light of the Palace" would now be called "Light of the World."

Such names had a very special meaning in that era. Kings regularly gave grand and poetic titles and names to members of the family or to courtiers, indicating their high status. In Jahangir's father's time, for example, senior women had sobriquets such as the Abode of Mary, the Great Lady of the Age, Liberality of Good Things, and Bounty of the House. Jahangir called royal matriarchs the Fortunate Lady, the Exalted Queen, and the Powerful Lady. The names he gave to his wives, concubines, and entertainers show his taste for beauty and opulence: the Mistress of Beauty, Bold-Eyed, and Pretty Body. His dancers and singers he dubbed Pearl, Ruby, Diamond, and Rose.

When Jahangir renamed his wife Light of the World, he elevated her onto even higher ground. Nur Jahan, Light of the World, conveyed brilliance, strength, and her status as the most important woman in the empire.

Nur was also given various land grants of her own, each estate known as a jagir. Having a jagir meant lucrative financial rights—to tax revenues, a share of profits from goods sold, and taxes on goods coming in.

> **Nur, Light**
>
> In Persian as well as in Pashtu, a language of Afghanistan familiar to the Mughals, "Nur" means "rock."

One such estate was Ramsar, twenty miles southeast of Ajmer, where the camp was pitched. Just after Khurram had gone to the Deccan, the Mughals spent eight nights in Ramsar. Jahangir fished and hunted gazelles, antelopes, and waterfowl. Nur looked after estate business, conferring with her treasurer. On the last night of their stay, she ordered a feast. On all sides and in the middle of a lake, upon a platform, lamps were lit. Gems, jeweled vessels, fine gold-beaded textiles, and a variety of other gifts were displayed before the emperor.

The sometimes sensitive, sometimes tempestuous and ill-tempered emperor was at home while traveling through the vast regions of his kingdom. Like a naturalist, he was absorbed in studying his land, its people, and its flora and fauna. Obsessed with gathering statistics, he ordered the measurement of all Mughal territories and their great range of animal, vegetable, and mineral resources. He had frequent discussions with clerics, astrologers, and poets.

Jahangir directed his generals and administrators. He put in a full imperial workday even when he was drinking or using drugs in the evening. But her husband's drinking and philosophical fixations on asceticism, art, scriptures, and the turmoil of human existence gave Nur unique opportunities to augment and implement her gifts of leadership. She began to finesse her hunting skills. Hunting was much more than a leisure activity. For Mughals, it symbolized dominance: stalking and shooting allowed a ruler to display his ability to tame the wild and to publicly assert his bravery in the open theater of the hunting grounds. Soon Nur would issue her first imperial order and save the property rights of her treasurer. She emerged as a vital presence in imperial ceremonies. Jahangir did not abdicate from his throne. But he approved of Nur's handling of government matters.

A new kind of rule was beginning to emerge in Mughal history. This was the first and only time when a pair of sovereigns ruled the empire. A man and a woman: Nur and Jahangir.

In 1617 the Mughals moved through the area of Malwa, roughly 330 miles southeast of the previous Mughal stop in Ajmer. Malwa was dotted with lakes, green valleys, stately palaces, and 360 notable Hindu shrines and temples. Willows and hyacinths lined the banks of calm rivers. Wheat, poppies, sugarcane, mangoes, melons, and grapes grew in abundance.

A celebrated and solitary ascetic, or holy man, named Jadrup was staying nearby. After many years of religious retreat in a far corner of the desert, the hermit had returned to this area. Jadrup was an expert on Vedanta, an ancient Hindu philosophy that holds that the human soul is part of the divine and stresses the harmony of all religions. Jahangir decided to visit him.

Jadrup lived in a tiny cave dug into the middle of a hill. The passage leading to the small pit where he sat was six feet long, three feet high, and just under two feet wide. The emperor braved the passage in order to talk with Jadrup in his cave. There was no mat, no straw.

As Jahangir explored matters of the spirit, Nur busied herself in hunting. On April 16, 1617, accompanied by the emperor, she set out on elephant-back to hunt. Her assistants used an ancient "battue" method of stalking. This was a regular practice on Mughal hunting parties. With the help of dogs, four tigers spotted by scouts were surrounded by beaters. The men pounded the bushes with sticks in order to drive the animals into a small open area.

The empress fired six shots and killed all four tigers.

Royal Hunting in the Mughal Era

Hunting revealed royal power: stalking and shooting allowed a ruler to display his talent to tame the wild and publicly assert his bravery.

During hunting trips, an emperor and his officers could also gather local intelligence and amass data about land revenue, trade, and production. A ruler had the opportunity to meet his people—peasants, for example, who might pay respects or make complaints.

A mighty Mughal hunting party might cause a disobedient or rebellious landholder to back down.

Hunting also disciplined, trained, and prepared armies for complex military operations.

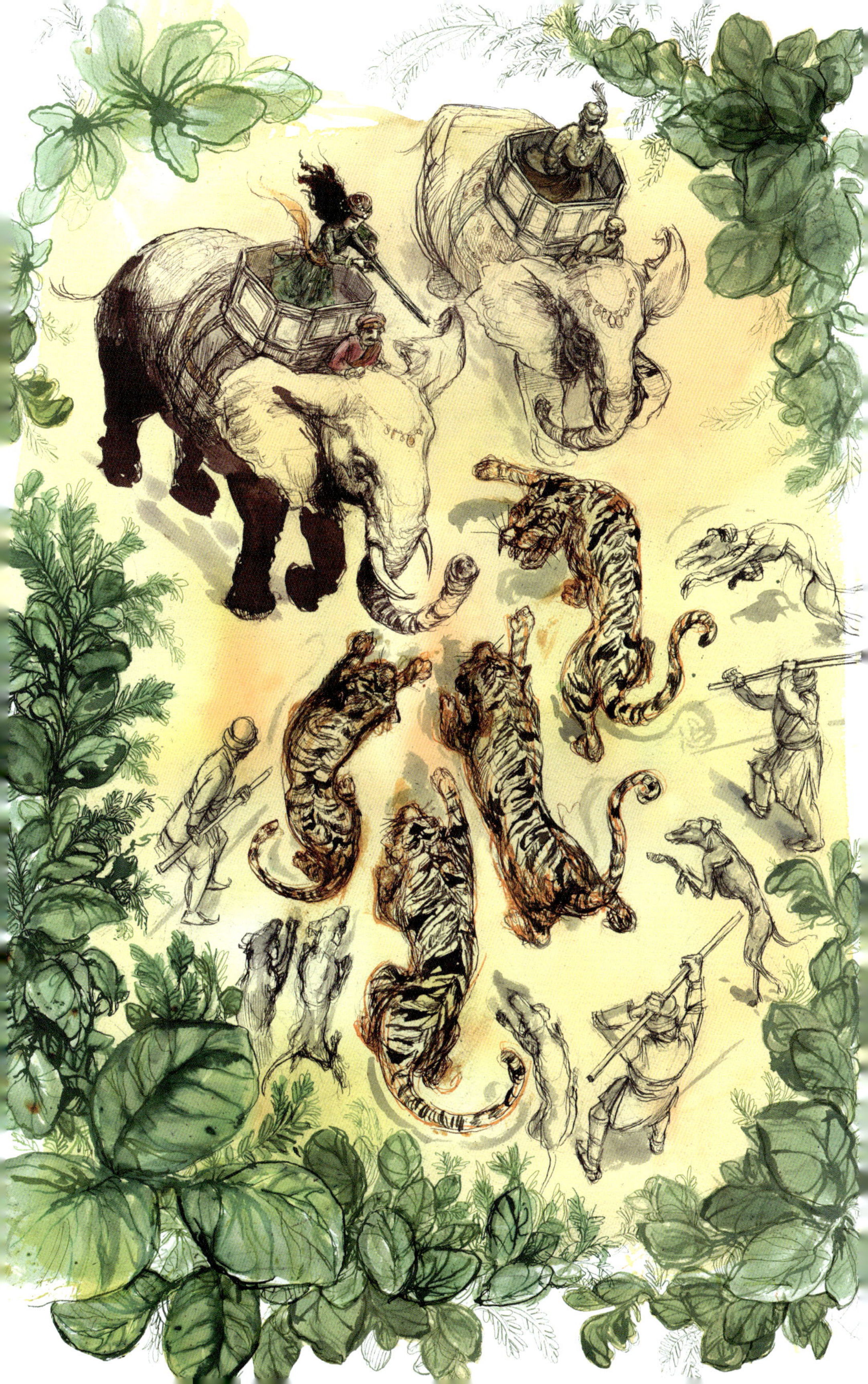

Jahangir was rapturous. "Until now, such shooting was never seen," he wrote. That "from the top of an elephant and inside of a howdah [her seat] six shots should be made and not one miss, so that the four beasts found no opportunity to spring or move." The emperor scattered coins over Nur Jahan.

A poet later wrote this couplet:

Though Nur Jahan be in form a woman
In the ranks of men she's a tiger-slayer.

That a woman could aim and shoot with such accuracy stunned this poet. He was not alone in his awe.

Six

NUR BECOMES CO-SOVEREIGN

As the Camp of Good Fortune moved through western India, Nur Jahan's dominance was on the upswing. She made decisions about her properties and commerce and taxes and took care of her poor subjects. She intervened to protect peasants from harassment or overtaxation by local authorities. Deeply compassionate, the empress supervised the care of little Prince Shuja, the epileptic son of her niece, who was pregnant for the third time.

In the summer after the tiger hunt that made Nur's reputation as an extraordinary markswoman, an emissary arrived at the Camp of Good Fortune. The Deccan campaign was going well, his missive said. Several leaders had surrendered, turning over the keys to their strongholds. The only troubling note: Malik Ambar hadn't yet surrendered.

Nur was the first to receive this encouraging news, which she brought to Jahangir. As a reward, the emperor gave Nur another tract of land nearby, called Toda. It had several villages and one large town. From Toda alone, Nur earned a great deal of money. Ramsar, her other estate, was also profitable.

Nur was at the center of state and private ceremonies—holiday celebrations, seasonal festivals, imperial bazaars, weddings. She presided over some and gave gifts at many. Always, family members and courtiers paid respects to her. That August, when the rainy season lessened, the royals marked the day of the first revelation of the Quran. It was also the Rakhi festival, during which Hindu women tie threads around the wrists of their brothers or elder men to symbolize the strength of their ties. To celebrate the three coinciding holidays, the empress arranged a feast at her lakeside mansion on the Ramsar estate.

The following month Khurram returned; he had been gone for eleven months. Malik Ambar still commanded strategic forts, but overall, the emperor considered the Deccan project a success. The prince kissed the imperial ground of the camp. He then presented thousands of coins as an offering to his father and gave the same amount to the poor. The most potent public demonstration of praise that night was that the emperor gave his son the title Shah Jahan, King of the World.

Of late, every major event in the life of the Mughal Empire had been heralded by dual acknowledgment—one from the emperor and one from the empress. Next, Nur honored Khurram as a brilliant warrior-prince.

Nur's presents to Khurram were:

- a jeweled turban ornamented with rare gems
- a robe of honor adorned with jeweled flowers and precious pearls
- a sword with a jeweled scabbard strap
- a pearled turban
- a band of pearls
- a waistband with pearl beading
- two horses, one of which had a jeweled saddle
- a royal elephant

> An unnamed court artist memorialized the meeting with a painting titled *Jahangir and Prince Khurram Feasted by Nur Jahan.*
>
> The empress is dressed in delicate light-ochre top and trousers, with a transparent stole over her shoulders. She wears a pearl-and-ruby necklace, earrings, and bracelets. Khurram, Nur, and Jahangir sit together on a raised carpeted platform, with the prince a bit below his father and stepmother. He is confident in his posture, yet smaller than the emperor and the empress.

Khurram, now Shah Jahan, was aware that Nur, along with her father, had been key in orchestrating the Deccan campaign. Three weeks after his return, he presented her with gifts worth two hundred thousand rupees—an astronomical amount in those days. To his mother and other women, he sent sixty thousand rupees. The prince gave Nur three times what he gave all the other elder women. "Such offerings had never been made during this dynasty," wrote Jahangir. In this public show, the prince endorsed Nur as co-sovereign.

Courtiers and Mughal intimates deferred to Nur's growing role in state decisions. But some members of the court began to take issue with her ascent. An uncle of Jahangir's wrote him a letter in which he targeted the dominance of Nur and her family. Another person troubled by Nur's rise was Mahabat Khan, a loyal but temperamental military commander of the emperor's. He, too, was uncomfortable with the eminence of

TIGER SLAYER

the empress, because she was a woman. Mahabat held back his reservations about Nur, but not for long.

In the portable Mughal bazaar, set up at a decorous distance from the imperial encampment, people spoke about Nur's growing influence. One of them was Thomas Roe, the English ambassador, sent by King James I to secure trading rights in India. Distinguished visitors, such as Roe, stayed at inns close to the bazaar or in nearby towns.

Mahabat Khan

Roe was having trouble gaining access to Jahangir and Nur. So he tagged along with the merchants and other camp followers: barbers, physicians, tailors, launderers, blacksmiths, weapons dealers, musicians, and food vendors, some of whom ran tea shops and tented guesthouses.

For help in reaching the empress, Roe turned to a fixer and translator, a man with the name of Jadu, which means "magic." Finally, Roe's official

Thomas Roe

seal was sent to the tented Mughal court. Roe was miffed when his diplomatic credential, having been kept overnight, was returned without the expected official invitation for an audience. He blamed Nur for what he considered a disrespectful and arrogant act. Roe wrote disapprovingly of Nur's power, saying that although the emperor had "more than a thowsand" women, "yet one governs him, and wynds him up at her pleasure."

This woman of verve and imagination definitely had state power on her mind. Within six years of her marriage, Nur had begun to show irrefutable signs of dominance.

She issued her first royal order in December 1617, just when the Mughals were considering returning to Agra. The emperor decided that since he'd never seen the ocean, he'd visit the coast before heading back to the capital. Nur didn't accompany him. Instead, she went to Toda, to rest, hunt, write poetry, and supervise the officers who looked after her properties.

There, the treasurer of her estate, a man named Baroman, was in trouble. His private money was being held by an officer of the raja of Bikaner, a city in India's western desert. Nur ordered the raja to ensure that payment to her treasurer be made immediately. The paper scroll bearing the order was adorned with a beautiful arch-shaped wax seal with the empress's signature:

Nur Jahan Padshah Begum or Nur Jahan,
the Empress of the Age

She signed as *Padshah*, meaning "sovereign" or "monarch." The same term that appeared alongside Jahangir's name.

In the past, royal women had signed orders as "mother of," "daughter of," or "sister of." Nur, however, was the first to issue orders in her own right. Her orders were not different from her husband's. They were about debt and revenue collection, land grants, military affairs, criminal cases, and protection of people such as her treasurer.

This signature was a public announcement that she was assuming the role of co-sovereign. With her husband's full approval.

Was Women's Rule Legally Accepted Back Then?

Among the Mughals and their itinerant ancestors, the idea of a daughter succeeding her father was not excluded, though it never actually happened. Nur was breaking ground. Born to foreign parents, she was not of the Mughal bloodline, hence no daughter of the dynasty. And yet no other Mughal woman had shown the power she did.

About the time that Nur started signing decrees, new kinds of gold and silver coins began to circulate with the emperor's name on the front and the empress's on the reverse. It was the first time that a woman's name had appeared on a Mughal coin. There were even some coins with Nur's name alone. The power of the empress was obvious to those in the royal household who received these coins as gifts. Other folks would notice, too, such as salt makers or cumin traders who brought their products to the Mughal court from far away and received these coins in payment.

Jurists, clergymen, and courtiers accepted edicts and coins as *technical* signs of authority—meaning that the empress's power was endorsed by law.

But there were also informal signs of being a ruler. The law didn't say much about such symbols of power, but these were hugely respected actions of a Mughal ruler. Hunting, to take an example, which we know Nur was outstanding at.

There was also the daily practice in which the emperor appeared in one of the decorated balconies (*jharokha*) of the palace to give his public a view (*darshan*) of himself. So the viewing was called: *jharokha darshan.*

Balconies projected from several sides of the palace or tent walls. It was a Hindu practice that Nur's father-in-law had instituted and her husband had adopted.

Now Nur appeared where no other Mughal queen had before, or would after. The empress showed herself on a balcony, at a distance, like a goddess. People gathered below. Getting a look at her was auspicious. Nobles presented themselves below the balcony "and listen[ed] to her dictates," wrote one court historian. "At last her authority reached such a pass," he added, that "the King was such only in name. . . . Repeatedly he gave out that he bestowed the sovereignty on Nur Jahan Begam."

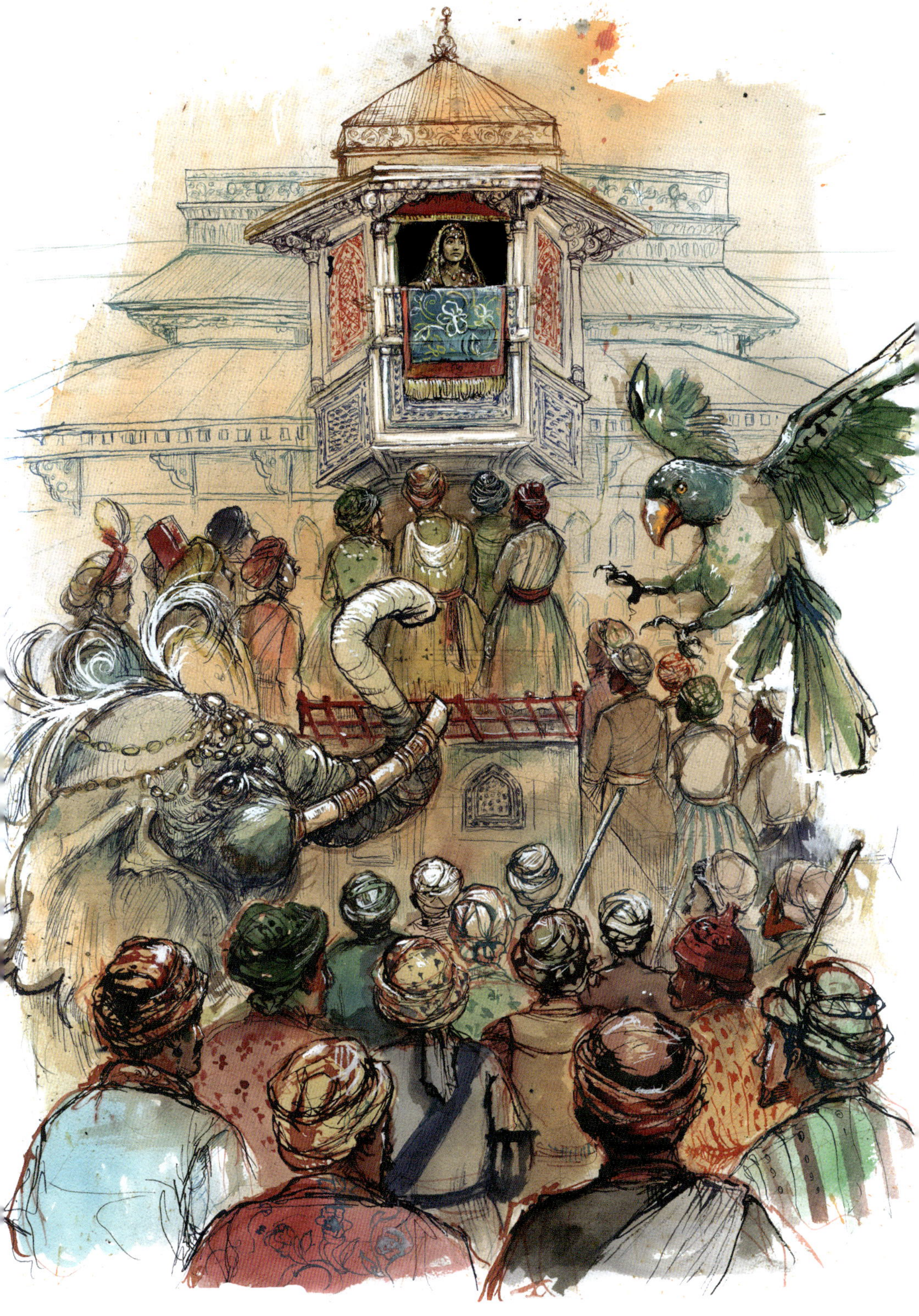

Seven

PORTRAIT FOR AN EMPRESS

It was the autumn of 1619. The days were clear and cool, perfect for travel. The royals had returned from western India some months prior. After her hectic travels and constant imperial engagements, the empress was weary. The emperor began thinking about a pleasure trip to Kashmir, as a restorative for his beloved Nur. He had been there twice with his father. He often described it as the garden of eternal spring. We can imagine Jahangir telling Nur about the beauty of Kashmir, its countless waterfalls, the sweet-smelling roses, violets, and narcissi, the views of lofty peaks.

And so, the royal cavalcade of the emperor and empress set out again from Agra, headed toward the tall Himalayas. Queen Mother Harkha and other royal women were in the procession. So were Prince Shah Jahan, as well as the empress's elderly father and brother and nobles, officers, stewards, attendants, servants, and soldiers. Mahabat Khan, the loyal general, recently appointed governor of Kabul, escorted the cavalcade part of the way.

Traveling one stage behind the main convoy was Khusraw, the former rebel prince. At Nur and Harkha's urging—and after listening to advice from the holy man Jadrup—the emperor had reconciled with his eldest son. Shah Jahan was watching his older half-brother closely for any sign that he was interested in succeeding to the throne.

A popular pilgrim site along the route was Mathura, littered with temples of the playful god Krishna and his consort Radha. The people of Mathura anxiously waited for the Mughal party. For months, a tiger had been attacking villagers and visitors, then disappearing into the forest. Men and women in Mathura knew that an emperor could solve the problem.

> **Killing tigers had long been a royal prerogative, reserved for kings and their families and a familiar sign of their power.**

According to one excited observer, the procession had nearly "fifteen hundred thousand" (one and a half million) people, and ten thousand elephants and a great many armaments soon arrived.

Attendants began erecting hundreds of stunning tents, with the harem quarters marked with beautiful carved red screens. A group of local huntsmen appeared, paid their respects to the

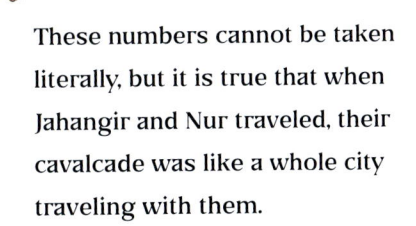

> These numbers cannot be taken literally, but it is true that when Jahangir and Nur traveled, their cavalcade was like a whole city traveling with them.

emperor, and begged him to do something about the killer tiger.

The emperor declined. He had taken a vow that he would give up hunting when he turned fifty. He'd promised Allah that he would injure no living being with his own hands. Now, two months past his fiftieth birthday, he had recently renewed his vow, as an offering to the gods on behalf his favorite grandson, four-year-old Shuja, who suffered from epilepsy. It was said in those days that if you gave up a favorite thing as an offering to the gods, a seriously sick person would be cured. Shooting a tiger was now out of the question for Jahangir.

But the tiger-slayer empress was there. Just two years earlier, she'd amazed her husband and his courtiers by slaying four tigers with only six shots.

On October 23, 1619, the beautiful and accomplished Nur Jahan mounted an elephant and settled into the elaborate seat on its back. She wore a regal turban, much like the ones favored by the emperor and noblemen, but highly unusual for a woman, and a knee-length tunic with a sash around the waist over tight trousers. Holding a tall musket, she looked stunning, with delicate earrings and a necklace of rubies, diamonds, and pearls. Her shoes were open at the back, exposing the henna designs on her feet.

The elephant handler led the empress along a sandy track toward the forest. Jahangir went on his own elephant, decorated with marigold garlands. A long line of courtiers followed. Some rode elephants or horses, while others walked alongside the attendants and local folks.

Local hunters on foot guided the party past fields of barley, peas, and cotton, lush from the recent rains. Along the way, they spotted herds of cattle, goats, and blackbucks with long corkscrew horns. When they reached the forest, the empress could barely see beyond the dense wall of creepers, bushes, and trees—lofty neem, thorny *babul*, and many others. The hunters showed the Empress and her retinue the spot where the tiger was likely to appear. They waited.

Soon Nur's elephant, in the lead, began groaning and stepping nervously from side to side. Her seat lurched precariously. From his own elephant, Jahangir looked on, silent and focused. "An elephant is not at ease when it smells a tiger," the emperor later wrote, and "to hit with a gun from a litter is a very difficult matter."

The tiger emerged from the trees. Nur lifted her musket. Aiming between the animal's eyes, she pulled the trigger. Despite the swaying of her elephant, one shot was enough. The tiger fell to the ground, killed instantly.

Jahangir was delighted. A woman shooting with such a large audience was highly unusual. A woman shooting with such expertise was unheard of.

Which of Nur's stirring performances would make the best portrait? This was the challenge the famous painter Abul-Hasan faced. What was most alluring? Her presence on a royal balcony, where she appeared like a goddess? The stunning gifts she gave? Her masterly hunting? What would best convey her delicacy, strength, and power?

The celebrated painter Hasan was seeing Nur's life unfold before his eyes. Lately, Nur was engaged in designing her first public building, an inn for travelers. Located in the city of Jalandhar, the inn sat on the Grand Trunk Road between Agra and Lahore. Meant to be a lodging for male travelers in the highly lucrative international trade, the inn could house up to two thousand guests, along with their camels and horses. It had a separate area for the imperial couple, and its own mosque. On the gateway of the inn, decked with sculpted animals and mounds of lotuses, Nur ordered an inscription in four rhyming verses. The last line was:

This saray [inn] was erected by Nur Jahan Begum.

Visitors couldn't miss the fact that the empress was the patron and creator of this grand inn. In act after act—hunting, advising, issuing orders, appearing on coins, designing buildings—Nur ensured that the public and posterity would remember her name.

Hasan had lived surrounded by art. He was the son of one of the most prominent men in Mughal art, an Iranian named Aqa Reza. When the empire was still in its infancy, the second Mughal emperor had invited Reza to his court, which was then based in Kabul. Reza trained several Mughal artists, including his son.

Hasan, a slight young man, started painting in his early teens. He drew European and Persian images and experimented with color. He showed that carefully painted folds of clothing could make the humans in his artwork look like they were living and breathing people, rather than flat figures. He painted sages, pilgrims, and, many times, the emperor himself. Hasan's painting of the emperor's accession became the frontispiece of the memoirs of Jahangir.

    Jahangir declared Hasan "Wonder of the Age."

Mughal women in paintings were always stunning, bedecked beauties. Commoners—singers, dancers, servants—were all painted in the same way, their faces identical, artificial. But none of these depictions—women in ornaments, as aged advisers, or as vessels of royal birth—would be right for Nur Jahan. The Mughal world had never known a woman like her.

How to express not only Nur's beauty and charisma but also the growing boldness of her leadership, buzzed about in the bazaar and among officials and visiting diplomats? A new kind of woman required a new kind of portrait.

The result was a dazzling portrait of the empress loading a musket—not just holding one. This is a rare example of action in a portrait of a royal woman. We don't know whether she posed for Hasan or he painted from sightings and his experience of Nur as a leader, defender, and hunter. Her confident posture implies that she was skilled with this weapon used in hunting and war. Groundbreaking in style and content, Hasan's portrait is radiant with energy.

Portrait of Nur Jahan Holding a Musket

The empress stands confidently, loading a musket. The gun is taller than she is, but Nur handles it with ease, tamping down gunpowder with her raised right arm. She's dressed in hunting clothes: a knee-length tunic tied with a sash, tightly fitting trousers, and a regal turban. She wears her famous ruby-and-diamond earrings. Her chin is up, her slender shoulders are back, and her chest is rising slightly. She looks into the distance, proud, full of vigor, bold, and free. Regal and commanding.

According to Mughal art experts, Hasan finished this work sometime between 1612 and 1617. He worked in a very small space, using just seventeen inches by twelve inches of paperboard. On it, he painted the full figure of the empress and surrounded her with fourteen delicate flowers in red, black, yellow, and blue.

Hasan gave us a rare picture of Nur Jahan's power. He put his name on the painting. Mughal artists didn't always sign their work. Hasan validated what everyone was seeing. The remarkable Nur Jahan, a woman who'd been the emperor's wife only since 1611, one of many, was now the empress of Mughal India. A Wonder of the Age herself.

Eight

DELAYED HONEYMOON

The empress had skillfully dispatched the killer tiger, earning the gratitude of her subjects and the admiration of her husband. The royal camp was pitched not far from the cave of the ascetic Jadrup. Before heading north toward the mountains, the emperor visited him once again. Only then did the royal procession go on to Delhi, making a stopover that lasted two and a half weeks. There they paid their respects at the tombs of Jahangir's grandfather and a Sufi saint. They visited the seventy-one-year-old former chief supervisor of the harem. Dai Dilaram, the empress's confidante, was now the head of the harem.

This was a pleasure trip after the years Nur and Jahangir had spent in western India, a much-delayed honeymoon. Royal family members; nobles, such as the strict and stocky Mahabat;

and the gentle paymaster and historian Mutamad Khan were in the retinue. They stopped at various places, visited shrines and gardens, and received distinguished nobles. The empress's niece Arjumand, the wife of Shah Jahan, had recently given birth to her seventh child, a boy. One of her older sons, the epileptic prince, traveled in the care of the empress.

Mughal officers ensured that the royals were comfortable as the road began to climb through the Himalayas. Reaching into their final destination, the city of Srinagar, would take a total of 168 days. The city magistrate of Agra went ahead with a group of stonecutters, carpenters, and shovelers to fix bumps, ruts, and potholes in the roads. They made the way easier for the wagons and the animals carrying loads. Local grandees would extend hospitality to the royals.

A place called Pakhli was the beginning of Kashmir territory. Advance scouts reported that because Kashmir's harvest of wheat and other grains had been meager that year, the villages ahead wouldn't be able to supply enough to feed the large number of elephants traveling with the Mughals. Jahangir sent all but seven hundred of the animals back to Agra.

Meanwhile, in the Deccan, where Shah Jahan had gone to war three years earlier, Ambar was still resisting Mughal rule. Jahangir, Nur, Ghiyas, and Asaf considered the steps to be taken. Shah Jahan, they decided, would again march to the south.

But Shah Jahan refused to head the military operation unless he could take along his eldest half-brother, the former rebel Prince Khusraw. He wanted to keep an eye on him, curtailing any ambitions he might have for the Mughal throne. Jahangir agreed. Shah Jahan left with his partially blind half-brother for a renewed campaign.

Meanwhile, Mahabat went on a tirade about the empress. He was about to return to his post of Kabul and decided it was time to complain to the emperor that Nur's control of imperial affairs wasn't a fitting arrangement. He told the emperor that many others felt the same way. He specifically mentioned the doubts expressed by a poet known to Nur and Jahangir. His Majesty must have read the histories of the ancient kings, the poet said, adding, "Was there any king so subject to the will of his wife? The world is surprised that such a wise and sensible Emperor as Jahangir should permit a woman to have such great influence over him."

For a few days, the emperor was reserved toward his beloved Nur. But as soon as they reached a spring and waterfall near Hasan Abdal, Mahabat departed toward Kabul, as planned. The emperor softened. Critics of his favorite wife were no longer in sight.

The Mughal procession continued on the most treacherous part of the journey.

It was clear that the entire camp wouldn't be able to travel together. Elderly Queen Mother Harkha, some of the harem women, and their attendants were to stay a few days longer at Hasan Abdal. The rest of the royal party traveled on in smaller groups. An advance camp—a few nobles, the chief steward, and workers—would cross the mountain passes first, preparing the way. A second set of nobles followed with the empress's father, Ghiyas. Then came the core Mughal camp: Nur, Jahangir, the empress's brother Asaf, the paymaster and historian Mutamad, some other nobles, a few harem intimates, servants, and select attendants.

Because of the high prices that were making it difficult to feed the humans as well as the animals, the huge numbers of courtiers, workmen, servants, and soldiers traveling with the Mughal party went back. Only those absolutely necessary went forward.

Thus, split into smaller groups, they traveled toward the most breathtaking mountain areas. They cut through a high pass and arrived at a waterfall on the Bahat River, where they drank wine in the shade of the trees. The management of the journey from this point on was in the hands of Mutamad. He went on ahead to prepare.

The road was dangerous and risky. Elephants were no longer suitable. The Mughals went on horseback. Up ahead loomed the Bhuliyas Pass, one of the toughest and narrowest of the journey. Jahangir gave orders that the camp should split again.

Dressed in warm sheepskin coats, Nur and Jahangir neared the pass, along with their entourage—the men on horseback, the women carried in palanquins. Soon, they ran into a snowstorm. Mutamad, who had gone in advance of the royal camp, had erected tents near the Bhuliyas village. Nur and Jahangir were able to take shelter. They spent a few days with warm fires, food, and rest.

They continued to cross the passes for another week. At long last, the group with Nur and Jahangir arrived at broader roads that led to the meadows of the Kashmir Valley. The air was chilly but cheerful with early blossoms—roses, sandalwood flowers, violets, hollyhocks, narcissi. There were unusual flowers like the *bulanik*, which had green leaves growing in the middle of its blooms. Jahangir was ecstatic: "The flowers of Kashmir are beyond counting and calculation. Which shall I write of? And how many can I describe?"

At Baramula, a major stop on the river Bahat, it is said that Nur Jahan bathed in a waterfall. Before they moved on, the emperor dubbed it Nur's Waterfall.

They were now thirty-five miles away from Srinagar, the chief town of Kashmir and their final destination.

Srinagar was laced with the refreshing scent of clover. Peach, almond, pear, and apple trees were in blossom; gateways, walls, courtyards, and houses blazed with tulips and jasmine. A sturdy stone palace-fort, built on a hill called the Hari Parbat, overlooking the lovely Dal Lake, became their residence. The lake was approximately four miles long and three miles wide and was fed by a channel that brought water from the mountains.

The waters of Dal Lake mirrored the fantastic fireworks arranged in Nur and Jahangir's honor. Legends say that

Jahangir ordered massive, maple-like *chinar* trees from Iran and planted them to please his beloved wife. The royal couple took trips around the city and its gardens, admired the flora and fauna, received guests. There was a sense of ease in the times.

A Persian poet, a regular presence at gatherings in Ghiyas's home when Nur was a girl, was living in Srinagar. He was now one hundred years old. When he visited the Mughals, the emperor honored him as the "King of Poets."

Twenty-four years earlier, a man named Haidar Malik had served Nur Jahan in the aftermath of her first husband's death. She had spent the required forty days of mourning in his house before going to Agra. He now lived ten miles south of Srinagar and came to renew his loyalty to the emperor and empress. They went partridge hunting among the flowing streams and lofty trees near his village. The couple was very pleased with the place. Taken by their delight, and to honor the happy moment of their visit to his home, Malik asked that the name of his village be changed. Jahangir renamed it Nurpur, City of Light.

And so the weeks went by. They drank wine and ate Kabul peaches. In these sensuous surroundings Nur may have read to Jahangir a flirtatious poem she's supposed to have written:

> *There is a ruby button on your silken robe*
> *You have been afflicted by a drop of my blood!*

Thirty-five years after the Mughal couple's visit, François Bernier, a French physician and philosopher, visited Kashmir. He was the first European to take the trip. In his book *Travels in the Mogul Empire*, he wrote that the ponds contained "fish so tame that they approach upon being called. . . . The largest have gold rings, with inscriptions, through the gills, placed there," he added, by the celebrated Nur Jahan.

However delightful their sojourn, Nur had a serious matter to deal with. A particular question had long weighed on her mind: Which of the Mughal princes should marry her daughter, Ladli? Records do not clarify why Nur wanted her daughter to marry one of the princes, as opposed to someone else. It is clear, though, that she wanted her daughter to live in the Mughal royal household.

Shah Jahan, the presumed heir—politically savvy, fiercely ambitious—was already married to Nur's niece. And to two other women before her.

Nur noticed that since his marriage with her niece, Shah Jahan had fathered children only with Arjumand. She was clearly his favorite. If the empress married her daughter to him, she would likely be a second-rank, subordinate wife.

> Like his father, and other predecessors, Shah Jahan had more than one wife. This was the way of the court culture.

It was increasingly clear to Nur that if he were to become emperor, the ambitious Shah Jahan would undermine her power. With him on the throne, she might have no imperial future at all. She needed to think carefully about choosing a royal husband for Ladli, one who might rival Shah Jahan to become the next emperor, and who would preserve her power.

Late in the autumn, the imperial banners turned toward Lahore, where they would stop on the way back to Agra. As far as the royal party could see, there stretched a natural carpet of saffron. The Mughal caravan stopped at some of the same spots where they had paused on the journey to Kashmir. As before, the core camp halted at passes that were exceptionally difficult and rough to cross. Jahangir had difficulty breathing.

The royal party reached Lahore in a month. Messengers brought news that in the Deccan, enemy soldiers were destroying fields and pasturelands. The Mughal forces had retreated, exhausted and short of resources. Shah Jahan traveled to Lahore for a brief visit, a strategy session with Jahangir, Nur, and their inner circle.

Jahangir's shortness of breath continued to worsen. The

question of Mughal succession seemed urgent. Nur never broached the subject of Ladli's marriage with Shah Jahan or his half-brother Parvez, the alcoholic prince. Khusraw, partially blinded and married, wasn't a good prospect, either.

Ultimately, Nur chose the youngest son, Prince Shahryar, as her daughter's husband. He was a last resort, a long shot, but a potential preserver of her power. Known for his good looks, he was patient and restrained — and easily manipulated.

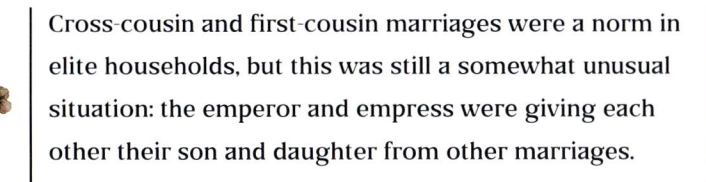

> Cross-cousin and first-cousin marriages were a norm in elite households, but this was still a somewhat unusual situation: the emperor and empress were giving each other their son and daughter from other marriages.

Mughal princes could be groomed as successors. If the right steps were taken and a prince had enough support, if he skillfully accomplished military and political assignments, he could become a contender for the throne. Nur knew well that it would be hard to keep Shah Jahan from the throne, but she decided she would take a chance and campaign for Shahryar as successor.

The emperor formally approached Ghiyas. He asked for his granddaughter in marriage to his son Shahryar. At an elaborate betrothal celebration at her father's impressive Lahore residence were Nur, a coterie of royal women, and the newly engaged pair themselves.

A rift quickly appeared between Nur and Shah Jahan. He was leaving for the Deccan. The emperor was weakening. Nur, at the center of the empire, was now closely tied to another prince who could easily become a contender for the throne. As Shah Jahan prepared to depart, his youngest brother, Nur's new protégé, occupied his mind.

Nine

BABY TAJ

The marriage ceremonies began soon after the Mughals returned to Agra in the spring of 1621. Nur's brother Asaf invited the newly engaged young couple, the emperor and empress, and members of the family to a grand entertainment. Taking on this important role, he marked his niece Ladli's upcoming wedding by giving delicate gems, special fabrics, and offerings in cash to his guests.

Asaf was now the *wakil*, or the emperor's representative, the most powerful person in the Mughal Empire after the emperor and empress. And as an ally of his sister the empress, and of the emperor, he celebrated an important event in Ladli's life. This way, he showcased his loyalty. But he was also partial toward and fully behind Shah Jahan, his son-in-law. Court life in which family and politics merged demanded that he act gracefully and diplomatically.

Shahryar's grandmother, the elderly Harkha, hosted a henna party. Rituals of decoration with henna took place in both men and women's residences. Delicate designs on Ladli's hands and feet, her eyebrows, and her eyes were painted with kohl. The men were decorated, too, but the women's party was a more elaborate affair, with music and dancing.

At night, the servants lit lamps in the garden below the private hall of the Mughal palace. Boats adorned with candles, torches, and lamps lined the river. Fireworks displays sparked the sky.

Typically, the mother of a Mughal groom laid out jewels, gold and silver utensils, brocades, carpets, rugs, canopies, elephants, horses, and cash to give to court servants, princes, harem women, nobles, and relatives. Shahryar's mother, a concubine whose name we do not know, would follow the protocol. Grandmother Harkha may have joined her in laying out the gifts.

Mughal princes and nobles escorted Shahryar from his residence to the palace. He kissed the ground before his father.

> Ladli was the third woman from Ghiyas's family to marry a Mughal: his daughter Nur had married the emperor; his granddaughter Arjumand had married Shah Jahan; and now his granddaughter Ladli was to be married to Shahryar.

Jahangir blessed him and gave him a robe of honor, a jeweled dagger, a sword and strap, a rosary of pearls, horses from the royal stable, and elephants with silver trappings. He fastened a veil around the prince's head, from which dangled strands of lustrous pearls, rubies, and emeralds. Dignitaries presented gifts to the prince.

Shahryar then mounted a horse with a gem-studded saddle and bridle. With rows of men on horseback, lines of garlanded elephants, foot soldiers with trays of wedding gifts upon their shoulders, the prince's entourage set out for Ghiyas's mansion. The bride waited there. After the prince departed for Ghiyas's mansion, the royals headed to the estate of Ladli's grandparents.

What did Ladli look like? No portraits of her survive, but it's possible to imagine her as a young version of Nur, strong-willed, with almond-shaped black eyes. As for Shahryar, a sketch made in preparation for a painted portrait shows that his face was delicate, his eyes small, and his gaze tender.

Under ordinary circumstances, as the bride's mother, Nur would have been by Ladli's side during the wedding. But she was also the empress. She sat with the emperor on a gold-embroidered divan. Hangings embroidered with silken gold threads and strings of pearls surrounded them. Persian carpets covered the floors. Grandmothers Harkha and Asmat would sit beside Nur. Slightly behind them, on cushioned divans, were Nur's sisters, the wives of her brothers, and her niece Arjumand. In a smaller part of the wedding area, tucked away from the public eye, Ladli was surrounded by women friends, female relatives, and Dai Dilaram. On the emperor's side, Shahryar, Ghiyas, Asaf and his brothers, distinguished nobles, and officers took their places according to rank. Musicians and sweet-voiced reciters performed wedding poems and songs. The officiating cleric pronounced the words of the marriage ceremony.

Ladli

A great feast followed. Grandfather Ghiyas presented rare gifts. A few days later, Nur celebrated in the Light-Scattering Garden, overlooking the river Yamuna: a pleasure garden with three descending terraces and walkways. In a royal entertainment, the empress presented great offerings to her son-in-law, showering him with jewels and precious goods. And thus, in public, she showed her support for the prince: he was now, without doubt, her most favored prince.

> The Taj. From the Light-Scattering Garden one could see the spot where one of the wonders of the world, the Taj Mahal, would one day stand. The Taj Mahal was Shah Jahan's tribute to Arjumand, who died during the birth of her fourteenth child in 1631. She is better known to the world by her imperial name Mumtaz Mahal, the Exalted One of the Palace.

In the Deccan, Shah Jahan kept up with the moves Nur made in favor of her son-in-law. He carefully assessed the possibility that his younger half-brother could emerge as a threat to his ambitions. He was not wrong to be suspicious. Contemporary nobles noted bluntly that the rift between Nur and Shah Jahan grew after Ladli's marriage.

Nur was at work bolstering her new son-in-law's prospects. She appointed a noted loyalist as a manager of Shahryar's household—that is, his chief of staff. The emperor himself appointed well-regarded officers as paymaster and finance officer to the prince's staff. Having such experienced and powerful figures with him would allow Shahryar to build his resources, as well as his reputation.

Eventually, Nur hoped, she would maneuver to have him lead an important military campaign. For a Mughal prince, getting a court rank and being married were symbols of becoming a mature adult. But these signs of princely adulthood did not make a man fully independent. He had to work in various offices to establish himself as a holder of power and a possible contender for the throne. The most significant thing was to get a key military assignment. Going to war, the big male domain, counted for a lot.

There was no news yet of a decisive victory from the Deccan. The emperor was agitated. His health deteriorated. The shortness of breath he'd experienced in Kashmir returned. One of the royal physicians applied gentle remedies, but to no avail. Another doctor implemented a more aggressive treatment. Nothing offered relief. A third doctor was called. He had been the chief royal physician in Persia and had migrated to India in the reign of Jahangir's father. Although he'd been honored as "the Messiah of the Age," even his treatment failed. With no relief in sight, the emperor became angry with the third doctor: "That ungrateful man . . . though he saw me in such a state, did not give me medicines or treat me." Everyone, including the emperor himself, knew that the problem was compounded by his drinking.

Finally, the empress took over. She reduced Jahangir's intake of wine and kept him away from unsuitable foods.

Jahangir recovered. Nur's skills and experience, he wrote, were "greater than those of the physicians . . . brought to bear through affection and sympathy."

Even though his improvement was temporary and it was evident that his health was beyond repair, Nur celebrated. At the next weighing ceremony, she arranged for an entertainment that was grander than usual. The servants hovered like moths around the emperor. The empress gifted them with sword belts, daggers, horses, elephants, trays full of money.

Two weeks later, the empress's mother, Asmat, died. The cause of her death is not known. "What can one write?" mused the emperor. ". . . No Mother of the Age was ever born equal to her." No husband, he went on, was equal to Ghiyas in his attachment to his wife. The emperor paid his respects to his grief-stricken father-in-law. Several days later, Ghiyas returned to public gatherings. He continued to look after the affairs of the empire and civil matters, yet in his heart he grieved.

At the end of October, Agra was unseasonably hot. Jahangir was keen to move to a more temperate region. So the court headed north toward hilly Hardwar, nearly 250 miles from Agra. A city revered by Hindus, it sits on the banks of the river Ganges. If the city wasn't to his liking, Jahangir said, they would head again toward Kashmir.

The core camp was made up of Jahangir, Nur, and Ghiyas—who was physically weak, in mourning—along with attendants and carriers of goods. With stopovers for hunting and visits to places along the way, it was mid-December by the time they reached Hardwar. Hermits and Brahmins, the learned pundits of Hinduism, thronged to receive alms in silver and gold coins. But no suitable place could be found for the imperial tents, so the Mughals went another two hundred miles farther north, to the area around Kangra.

Once settled, the party hunted, received officials, and granted awards. In a village along the way, Nur gave robes of honor to forty-five great nobles and intimate servants. Reports from the Deccan trickled in. Ambar continued to resist Shah Jahan's forces, and the blind Prince Khusraw had fallen ill.

Yearning to tour the fort and the hill country of Kangra, Jahangir set off with Nur and a group of courtiers and servants. Ghiyas stayed back, in the care of a top officer. They hadn't yet reached Kangra the next day when news arrived that Ghiyas's condition had deteriorated. There was little hope of his survival. Nur was distraught. The royals quickly turned back.

The dying Ghiyas went in and out of consciousness. Pointing at Jahangir, Nur asked her father, "Do you recognize him?"

As the sun set on January 27, 1622, three months and twenty days after his wife's death, one of the greatest nobles of the Mughal Empire passed away. Jahangir offered condolences to his sons and sons-in-law and gave forty-one of his children and grandchildren, as well as his clansmen and servants, dresses of honor and garments of mourning.

And then he did something unprecedented. Jahangir declared that everything belonging to Ghiyas Beg's establishment was to go to Nur, even though Ghiyas's oldest son, Asaf, and his other sons and daughters were alive. Her inheritance included Ghiyas's official positions and all the possessions related to his administration. The officers and staff attached to her father's office and household also went to the empress. The administrative bequest was the most important one: Jahangir had declared that Nur was, in effect, the successor of the great wazir—prime minister as well as empress.

Jahangir ordered that drums were to be sounded to announce Nur's arrival at court, as they had been for her father.

TIGER SLAYER

That year, Nur commissioned a garden tomb on the banks of the Yamuna to honor her parents. An exquisite four-sided building, it is made of white marble, semiprecious stones, colored mosaic, and latticework.

She called it I'timad ud-Daula's Tomb; although named after Nur's father's title, it houses both his and Nur's mother's crypts.

I'timad ud-Daula, which means "the Pillar of the State," was an honor conferred upon Ghiyas by his son-in-law Jahangir.

Nur Jahan built this memorial garden in a pattern that Babur, the first Mughal emperor in India, had begun. But she added her own flourishes: terraces and platforms. The crypts of her parents lie in ochre-colored memorials under an ornamental vault in the central chambers. The vault is richly painted with Persian images, such as rosewater vases, wine cups, lilies, and red poppies—there's a lot of red. Red flowers represented suffering and death.

This motif of the color red would appear in the famous Taj Mahal, built a decade later. Nur's garden plan with crisscrossing pathways would also appear on a grand scale in the Taj. The beautiful white marble with multicolored stones on the exterior of the mausoleum served as an inspiration for the Taj, as well.

A Jesuit missionary and geographer, a man named Josef Tieffenthaler, was in Agra in the 1740s. He found the tomb of Ghiyas and Asmat more attractive than the Taj Mahal. It surpassed all Agra monuments, he wrote.

Though rickshaw pullers and tour guides in Agra today call the tomb the "Baby Taj," in truth it is the Taj Mahal that is the baby of the memorial that Nur Jahan built for her parents.

Ten

ANARCHY

The year 1622 started badly and got worse. While the pain of Nur's father's death was still fresh, news came that Prince Khusraw had died in the Deccan. He was thirty-four. Shah Jahan had insisted on taking him south because he was suspicious of his ambitions. Many courtiers were certain that Shah Jahan had ordered his half-brother's murder. In his official report, Shah Jahan gave the cause of death as colic—that is, intestinal blockage.

Troubles unfolded one after another. By midwinter, the shah of Persia had amassed troops near Kandahar. His aim was to seize the massive fort there. Kandahar, Nur's birthplace, a rich commercial center at the border between India and Iran, had magnetic appeal. It sat on a major link on the trading routes traveled by merchants, mystics, and those seeking haven in India. Since the 1600s, the Mughals and the Safavids (the ruling dynasty in Persia) had clashed repeatedly over Kandahar, which was currently in Mughal hands. Often there were skirmishes between the two powers, but so far these had not flared into outright war. Now the situation was urgent. The troops of the Safavid emperor Shah Abbas seemed poised to attack Kandahar.

The Mughals would have to choose a commander for the campaign. This was not a simple decision. Getting the army to Kandahar wouldn't be easy. The long distance from Agra, and then the treacherous mountain passes they'd have to cross—part of the Sulaiman Mountains, whose highest peak reaches 11,700 feet—presented huge problems. In winter, snow blocked the passes. In summer, sweltering heat and scarce water threatened travelers. Spring was hardly better: torrents caused mudslides that blocked the narrow passes. Autumn, too, posed logistical problems. Since most camel herders headed eastward then, it would be hard to hire camels to go westward.

Meanwhile, Nur and the ailing Jahangir were troubled by Shah Jahan's aggressive behavior toward the empress.

From his base in the Deccan, he ordered a group of his soldiers to seize properties belonging to the empress and Shahryar in Dholpur, in western India. Some of these lands had once belonged to Shah Jahan but had been reassigned by the emperor to Shahryar. The man in command of the Dholpur garrison fought a brave battle, but he was overpowered by Shah Jahan's army. Men died on both sides.

Nur was furious; the conflict between her and Shah Jahan was evident for all to see. Jahangir, heartsore, recognized Shah Jahan's attack as the first sign of open revolt. He knew the omens all too well: he had once launched a similar rebellion against his father. And his eldest son had unleashed one against him. He ordered Shah Jahan, still fighting in the Deccan, to restrict himself to the lands he'd been assigned. He also asked him to send troops for the Kandahar campaign. The prince refused. Seized by debilitating shortness of breath, the emperor was distraught. "Of which of my pains should I write?" he lamented in his memoir, complaining of "such an undutiful son."

> Though Shah Jahan's rebellion distressed Jahangir, it didn't disqualify the prince from succession. A prince's rebellion was not a break in the order of the Mughal world: many princes rebelled against their emperor fathers, a rite of passage in a way.
>
> Court historians often downplayed the role of the princes and blamed individuals in the prince's or the emperor's inner circle. The underlying belief was that a prince was young and impressionable, inexperienced, easily misled.

With Shah Jahan out of favor, Nur moved to advance her son-in-law's fortunes. She proposed that Shahryar command the Mughal forces in Kandahar. Jahangir agreed. Experienced nobles and commanders joined his troops. The emperor upped Shahryar's rank and gave him more lands. Meanwhile, Ladli was pregnant. A potential heir might strengthen Shahryar's claim to the throne.

But discontent among members of the court was rising. Many felt that Shah Jahan's revolt was Nur's fault. She was believed to be overriding the emperor's orders. She "changed everything," wrote Farid Bhakkari. The conflicts, he declared, were due to the "mischief-making of Nur Jahan." The writer had praised Nur for her political skills, her artistry, and her generosity—but he still believed that a woman should rise only so far.

Nur knew that court deals and factions could twist, snap, and reconnect in surprising ways. Without her parents, who had been her closest supporters and advisers, and with her brother Asaf's loyalties uncertain, the political order she had established was at risk of fragmenting.

Though Nur and Jahangir were distressed by Shah Jahan's open hostility, Asaf remained silent. His sister and his

Asaf Khan

son-in-law were at loggerheads. Keeping silent was the way he dealt with this complex situation. Alarmed by her brother's apparent swing toward the rebellious prince, Nur summoned the emperor's trusted general Mahabat Khan from Kabul.

Mahabat had been hostile to Nur's family. He'd spoken out against Nur to Jahangir on the way to Kashmir. But he was also the emperor's longtime, much-tested supporter. He had turned against Shah Jahan over the death of the eldest son, the blind prince. Nur believed that Mahabat could be convinced to support Shahryar.

Mahabat wrote back to Nur Jahan that he wouldn't come to Agra if her brother Asaf was there. Mahabat suspected Asaf of secretly supporting Shah Jahan. He feared that because of his outspoken opposition to Nur's family, Asaf had marked him for death. He would come to court only if she dispatched her brother to Bengal, away from the center.

Rather than sending her brother to Bengal, Nur ordered him to transport gold and precious jewels in the royal treasury from Agra to Lahore. It looked like a fulfillment of Mahabat's request, and he came to the court.

For over a year, Shah Jahan and his men had fought his father's forces. They set up a base in the north of the Deccan, with plentiful supplies of wheat and millet, fertile pasturelands, and commercial wealth from busy trade routes. In the spring of 1622, Shah Jahan marched to Agra. He and his forces hoped to seize the treasury. The assault seemed well timed: Kandahar preoccupied the Mughal court.

Even so, the Mughal response was swift. When Shah Jahan reached the gates of Fatehpur-Sikri, not far from Agra, he found them shut. He ordered a confidant of his to take a contingent to Agra and confiscate whatever treasures they could find. The men entered houses, grabbed money and jewels. Eventually, Jahangir's soldiers chased them away and the treasury remained safe.

While the rebel prince and his forces were regrouping, the emperor sent him a message. He asked the prince to send the terms under which he would call off his rebellion. Shah Jahan's envoy brought a list of demands. Jahangir doesn't tell us what they were, only that he found them unreasonable. Most likely, the prince required restoration of his lands, and maybe a promise of the throne. Jahangir was enraged. He imprisoned the prince's representative.

Until the break between Nur and Shah Jahan was in the open, courtiers and critics had digested the rise of the empress. They accepted her edicts, coins, and sitting in the imperial balconies. But once she and Shah Jahan were publicly in opposition, courtiers began to condemn her character and speak of the dangers of her power. It was said that she sparked the fire of sedition. It was said that she had sown the seeds of dissension within the royal family. Shah Jahan himself accused Nur of being power hungry and blamed his father for allowing a woman to use such authority.

Later, court historians would use a severe label for Nur's power: *fitna*.

Fitna meant civil strife so profound that it was nothing short of cosmic disorder.

> Just after Prophet Muhammad died, his beloved wife Ayisha went into a battle against the contender for succession, Ali. He was the son-in-law of the Prophet. She led her forces against his in a fight known as the Battle of the Camel. In Islamic sources, this battle is said to be the first example of *fitna*—chaos or civil war. Some saw Ayisha as the champion of the rightful. For others, she was "mischievous," "worthless," and "ambitious." Wounded in battle, the defeated Ayisha was rebuked by the victorious caliph Ali: "Is that what the Messenger of God ordered you to do? Didn't he order you to remain quietly in your house?" For centuries after the Battle of the Camel, various Islamic sources associated *fitna* with destructive elements in women. Women were a source of trouble, turmoil, and temptation.

Jahangir wanted Shah Jahan as his successor. But he had an enlightened vision of his kingship. After all, he had Nur Jahan as co-ruler. Maybe the emperor had expected some kind of co-rule to continue after his death: Shah Jahan ruling the empire and Nur serving as his wise adviser and guiding light. Throughout Mughal history, women had served as counselors and guides. Nur was far more experienced in politics than any of those women had been.

But the emperor now knew that his wife and son would never share authority in any form.

The Mughals lost Kandahar. Nur and Jahangir were miserable about the loss, though probably not surprised. The campaign took place in late 1622. The heavy cannons that would have ensured victory would have to have been dragged through treacherous passes by thousands of bullocks and elephants. That was impossible during the season of snows. The Mughal troops could carry only lighter cannons. That put them at a great disadvantage against the army of the shah. The ill-prepared Mughal battalion surrendered.

Meanwhile, Shah Jahan continued to clash with his father's troops. Though Jahangir was in poor health, he insisted on setting out to confront his rebel son. In Punjab, for example, many officers who'd been serving under Shah Jahan came over to Jahangir's side; he promoted many of them to higher ranks. The emperor was pleased with the expansion of his forces. Twenty-five thousand men had gathered to fight the prince. Jahangir put Mahabat in command of the army and went back to Agra.

Shah Jahan's forces and Jahangir's army came face-to-face near Delhi. Mahabat sent a tactful message to Shah Jahan suggesting that if he returned to the Deccan, his landed rights and other privileges would be protected. The prince declined. Battle followed. Shah Jahan fled again. Short of resources and plagued by desertions, he retreated to a fortress called Asirgarh on an important route connecting the north and the south. A cousin of Nur's was in charge there. The empress sent orders to reinforce the bastion. But Nur's relative surrendered the fortress to the prince without opposition. Then Mahabat approached the fort of Asirgarh. Shah Jahan once again lost heart and retreated.

By November 1623, the prince had made his way to the eastern provinces—Orissa, Bengal, and Bihar—pursued by Mahabat and the imperial forces, which had been joined by Shah Jahan's half-brother, Prince Parvez. There he focused on gaining the support of groups that felt alienated from the Mughal center. Shah Jahan won them over by awarding them titles, land, and administrative appointments and built up his supplies of gunpowder, lead, iron, stone shot, and corn.

The end of Shah Jahan's open rebellion came near the town of Allahabad in late 1623. He had moved there and taken the riverside fort and all nearby boats. Mahabat and Parvez and their troops camped across the Ganges River from Shah Jahan. Nur and Jahangir followed the developments from Kashmir.

Shah Jahan's advisers warned him against engaging with the imperial forces, which far outnumbered his. The Mughal army had forty thousand skilled horsemen and foot soldiers. The prince's army barely numbered seven thousand. The prince sent the women of his harem to the nearby fortress at Rohtas for safety. Then he moved his troops seventy-five miles northwest of Rohtas to the city of Banaras. Mahabat followed him.

Among other members of the harem, Shah Jahan's wife Arjumand and his newly born son had been traveling with him all along. The harem always camped a good distance from any battles.

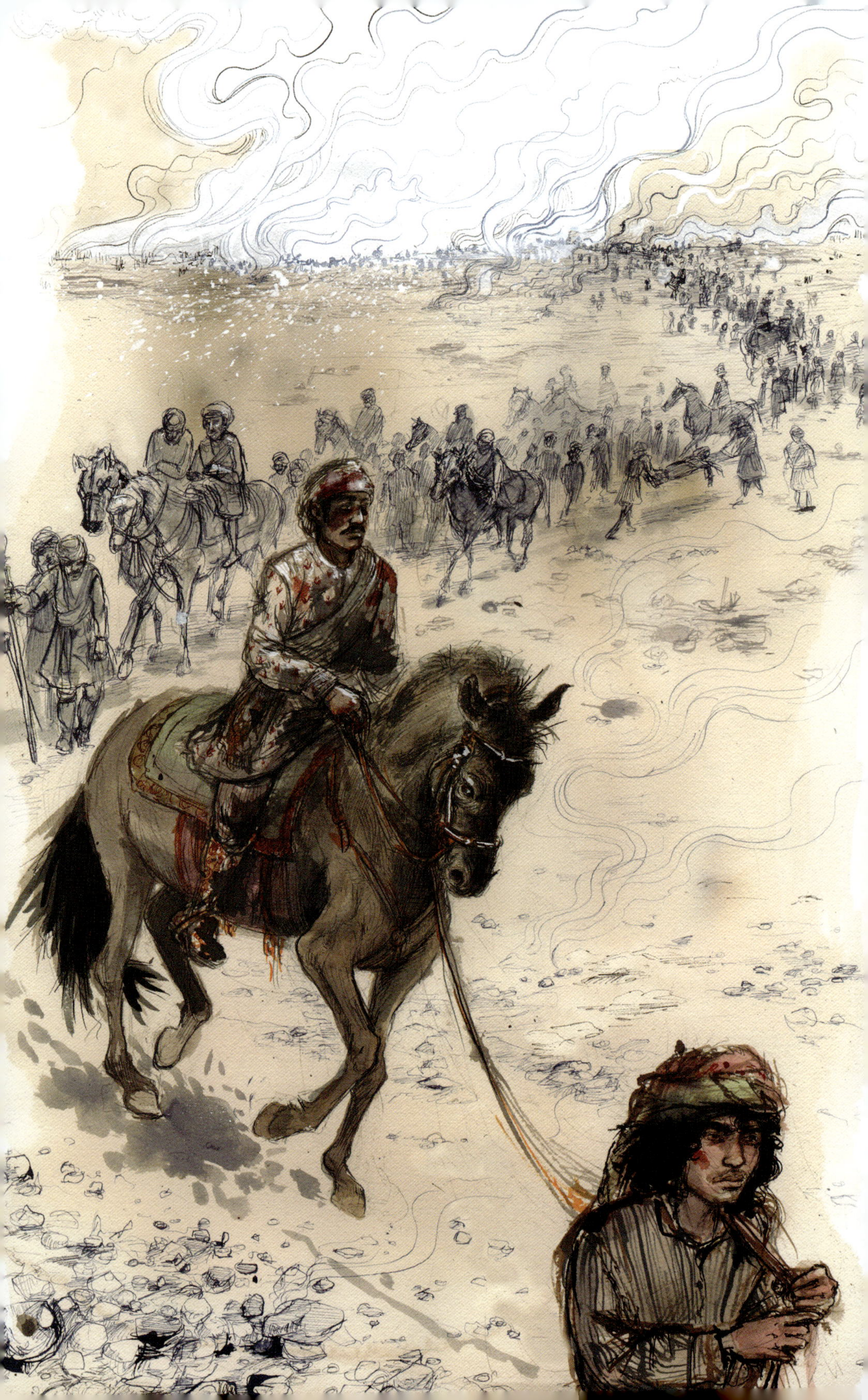

Shah Jahan arrayed his forces with himself in the center. Parvez and Mahabat assembled their troops. The Mughal artillery moved their heavy weapons forward and fired, the emperor later wrote, what sounded like a thousand cannon balls. The prince's forces crumbled. Many men were slaughtered on both sides.

A musket ball hit Shah Jahan in the head. Carried back to camp by his men, he sent a message to a trusted lieutenant ordering him to attack the imperial center with the few forces they had left. It would be wiser, the prince's lieutenant replied, to retreat from the battlefield and reassess the situation.

Shah Jahan mounted his horse. A servant led the wounded prince away. Mahabat and Parvez didn't pursue the defeated rebel—most likely on the emperor's orders. Though Jahangir was enraged at Shah Jahan, he would have wanted his son alive so that he could come to his senses, repent, and perhaps eventually take the throne.

Leaving his favorite wife and his infant son in the citadel of Rohtas, Shah Jahan retreated toward the Deccan, beyond Mughal control.

Eleven

A DARING RAID

It had been more than two years since Shah Jahan's defeat and the emperor's serious bout of breathlessness. In the spring of 1626, the empress and emperor were back on the road, traveling from Lahore to Kabul. Servants had raised the colorful tents of the vast imperial camp on both banks of the Bahat River. It was a wide body of water, swift, and fed by many tributaries.

On the quiet morning of March 16, Mahabat entered the lightly guarded tent compound. He and his men passed the harem tents, moving toward the emperor's rooms. At sword point, Mahabat kidnapped Jahangir, taking him and a few retainers to a site a few miles beyond the royal camp. Then he ordered his troops to burn the main bridge over the river, to thwart any rescue attempts from the other side, where most of the court's tents were pitched. The narrow makeshift bridge they erected in its place was closely guarded.

Later that day, two veiled women emerged from the harem tents and stepped onto the temporary bridge. The guards didn't give them a second look, and the pair passed to the other side.

After crossing the river in disguise, Nur and Jawahir Khan, her head eunuch, hurried to the camp of her brother Asaf. The empress immediately summoned a council of principal nobles and officers.

> ***Eunuch*** means a castrated male. From remote antiquity, eunuchs were employed in Europe, India, and China. They served as heads of guards in harems and as chamberlains to kings. In Mughal India, they were employed in some of the highest offices as loyal officers. Some rose to become bodyguards, confidential advisers, ministers, or generals.

Meanwhile, Mahabat realized that he had neglected to take the empress captive. By the time he became conscious of his folly, it was too late. She had already escaped across the river.

Why did Mahabat, until then steadfastly loyal, take the emperor captive?

Mahabat had failed to send the emperor a promised number of elephants and had held back a huge amount of money, part of the taxes and revenues taken from landowners that were supposed to be given to the royal treasury. Jahangir was further irked when he found out that Mahabat had married his daughter to the son of an eminent family without first asking him for the customary blessing. The son-in-law was publicly dishonored and thrown into prison, his gifts and cash were confiscated, and Mahabat's daughter was ordered to appear in court. Away in the south, Mahabat knew about none of this.

In early 1626, Jahangir had commanded Mahabat to appear at court with the elephants and the money he owed. Mahabat dispatched a messenger to the emperor saying that he had already sent the elephants. As to the money, he made various excuses for not delivering. Before heading to the Mughal traveling court, as the emperor had ordered, Mahabat tried to turn Parvez against his father. Nothing came of his attempt to conspire with the prince.

On his way, Mahabat found out that the emperor had arrested his son-in-law and ordered his daughter to appear in court. He considered all this a vile attack on his daughter's reputation, as well as his own. He also learned that Asaf had plans to imprison him when he caught up with the Mughal cavalcade. And so, along his route, he stopped to gather troops in Rajasthan, home of the Rajputs, a warrior class with whom he had strong political ties. A large contingent of Rajput soldiers vowed loyalty to Mahabat.

When Mahabat reached Lahore, Asaf sent him a humiliating order to pay the money he owed and produce the missing elephants before he'd be allowed to appear in the presence of the emperor at the royal encampment.

Mahabat's fury and fear surged. He told one of his trusted lieutenants to move ahead with a thousand men to protect the bridge over the river where he knew the royal cavalcade was camped. As a cover story, he sent a message saying this lieutenant was coming with his men to join the imperial army.

Asaf had indeed concocted a scheme to capture Mahabat. The idea was that Mahabat would pay his respects to Jahangir. The emperor would lead him onto a royal barge, where guards would hold him. Asaf believed that Mahabat didn't represent much of a threat. He certainly did not expect him to arrive with a large army. Asaf moved his camp, the traveling treasury and armory, and most of the imperial soldiers to one side of the river and left Jahangir on the other side. Only a small number of intimates, eunuchs, and servants stayed on with Jahangir. A few guards remained at the entrances and exits near the emperor and the harem, which included Nur's tents.

When Mahabat's spies reported that Asaf had left the emperor lightly guarded, he decided to act. He stationed a large number of men at the bridge. Accompanied by a hundred soldiers armed with spears and swords, Mahabat rode past the harem to the royal pavilion and alighted from his horse.

Paymaster Mutamad emerged from the pavilion. He warned Mahabat about the impropriety of approaching the emperor accompanied by soldiers. *Where is your etiquette?* he asked in Persian. He told Mahabat to wait until his presence was announced. Mahabat ignored him and strode to the door of the private bath, where his men began tearing down the boards that the doorkeepers had put up for security.

Mutamad hurried to the emperor and informed him about Mahabat's audacity. The emperor came out of the royal pavilion and went and sat on a raised platform, a sort of open-air throne. Mahabat saluted Jahangir, feigning submission. But as Mahabat spoke, more of his men rode up, fully armed.

Realizing his treachery, Jahangir twice placed his hand on his sword, as if to draw it. A noble standing by advised the emperor that the time was not right. Revealing his true purpose, Mahabat addressed the emperor. He instructed him to mount his horse as usual so that it would look as though he was riding out with Mahabat beside him. The emperor rode a distance of two arrow shots from the imperial pavilion—a few hundred yards—then switched without protest to a waiting elephant, which had knelt to allow him to mount.

Three trusted guards, biding their time, took seats surrounding the emperor atop the elephant. A celebrated surgeon, Muqarrab Khan, who was traveling with the royal cavalcade, also got into the seat on the elephant. Mahabat tried to chase him away by hitting him on the head with a stick. Jahangir's wine and bowl holder, whose name translates as "Soaked with Service," began climbing upon the elephant as it stood up. Mahabat's soldiers attempted to yank him down, but he held on, and the entourage moved forward with Soaked with Service dangling from the elephant. Despite the confusion, anyone who saw the emperor in the center of this hastily mustered retinue might think he was heading out to hunt.

In the hullabaloo, Mutamad slipped away, most likely to warn Nur about what was going on. When Mahabat realized that he had forgotten about the empress, he brought Jahangir back to the royal compound. But the empress was safely on the other side of the river. Mahabat then thought about Shahryar. Letting him stay free would be another great error. A Mughal prince, especially one who was Nur Jahan's son-in-law, could make big trouble. Mahabat took the emperor to Shahryar's tent, where he spent the night and the next day.

On the other side of the river, the bank opposite Jahangir's pavilion, Nur hurried to the tented quarters of her brother Asaf Khan. The empress immediately summoned a council of principal nobles and officers. She rebuked the council, her brother amid them. It was because of their inattention that the emperor had been kidnapped: "You have been disgraced . . . by your own actions," she said. "The best tactical plan is to array our forces tomorrow, cross the river . . . , overthrow the miscreants." All present agreed with the empress.

Mahabat allowed Jahangir to send Nur two messages. According to the poet Mulla Kami Shirazi, who wrote a lavish eyewitness account of these events, the first message expressed the emperor's misery at being separated from Nur. He asked her to come to him: "Without her the flower of my pleasure and delight has fallen down in pieces; and I have stuck to my skirt the thorn of her separation / And if she desires my safety she should start immediately and not quarrel with the circumstances."

Nur respectfully told the messenger that she was determined to conquer the "source of deceit and deception," as she called Mahabat. In a second message, the emperor urged the empress and her brother Asaf not to cross the river. A futile and hazardous battle might endanger him in captivity.

But Nur, Asaf, and the council of nobles proceeded. They knew that Jahangir was with Shahryar on the far side of the encampment. Crossing the deep, swift waters of the river in the presence of Mahabat's soldiers would be a challenge. But the overseer of the royal barge and inspector of ships concluded that there were sections of the river shallow enough to ford. Nur and the nobles drew up a detailed, careful plan for distributing their troops, horses, elephants, guns, and cannons.

On March 18, Nur perched atop a war elephant. Armed with a musket, she led a daring battle as commander of the Mughal forces that marched into the chilly waters of the Bahat River. Angry waves swirled around the elephants. Royal servants blew bugles. Armed with guns and swords, Asaf, his son, distinguished nobles, cavalry, camels, and hundreds of foot soldiers set off toward the opposite side of the river where a line of Mahabat's troops waited.

The chosen crossing turned out to be the worst possible place on the churning river. It had several stretches of deep water. When the men and animals hit these spots, their orderly advance turned chaotic. Asaf's son made it to the opposite shore, where he killed Mahabat's brother. Asaf feared that Mahabat might retaliate by killing the emperor. He withdrew from the battle and, with two hundred horsemen, bearers, and servants, retreated to a nearby fortress.

Nur, thinking that her brother was still with her, moved forward on her elephant. She drew close to the ranks of Mahabat's men. There was much tumultuous noise and commotion. In the uproar, Mughal cavalry and foot soldiers, horses and camels plunged into the turbulent water. Nur saw that Mutamad stood near a tributary conversing with another notable. Another eunuch in the service of the empress, a man named Nadim, went over to them with a warning: "Her Majesty wants to know why you have stopped to contemplate. Be brave, for as soon as you enter the battle, the foe will be routed." The two men rushed into battle.

Mahabat's army stood firm. Nur's forces were in disarray, struggling to keep from drowning. Waterlogged saddles and blankets dragged the horses down. But Nur advanced bravely. Her elephant received two sword wounds on its trunk. Two spears cut gashes in its back. The handler of Nur's elephant

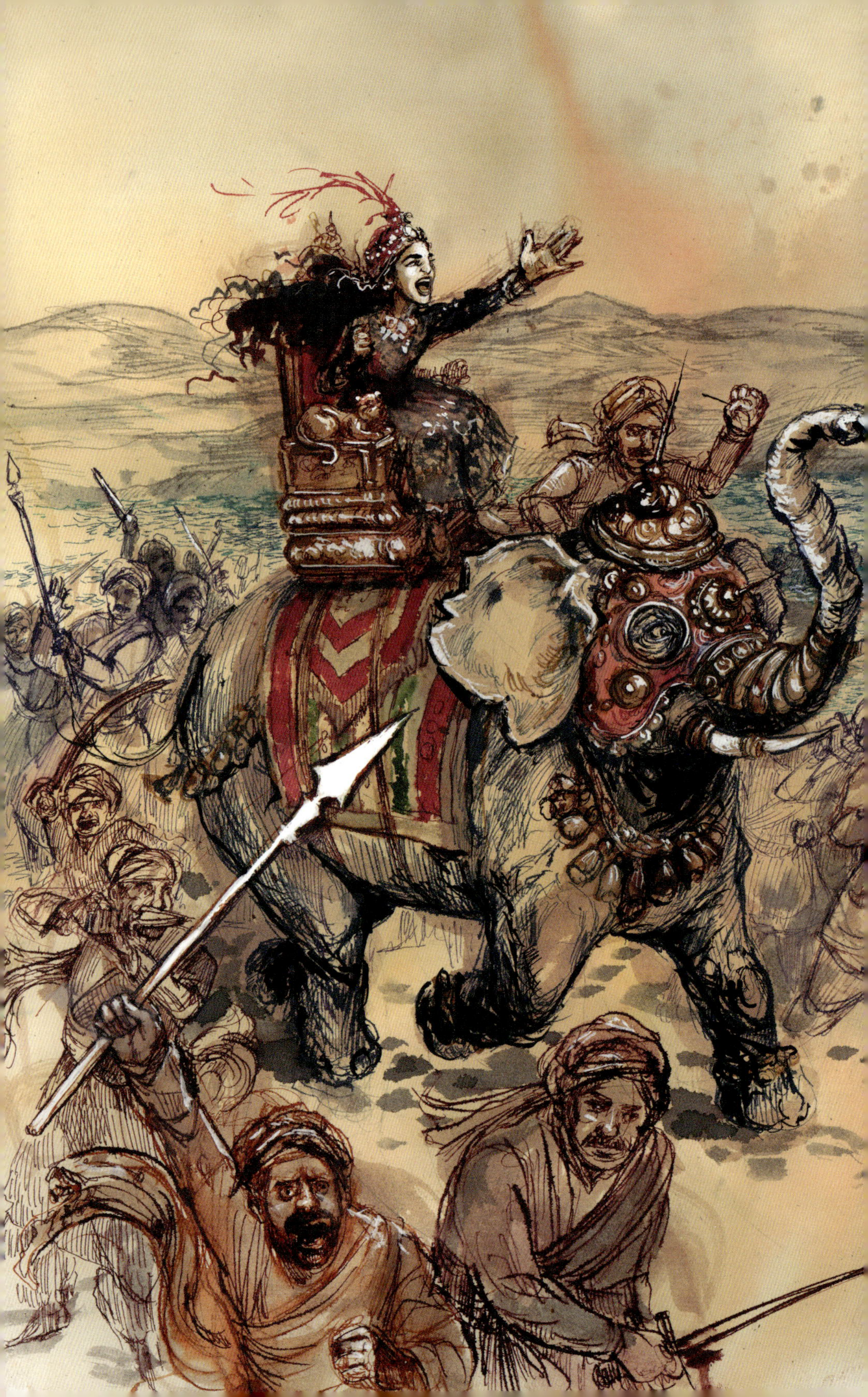

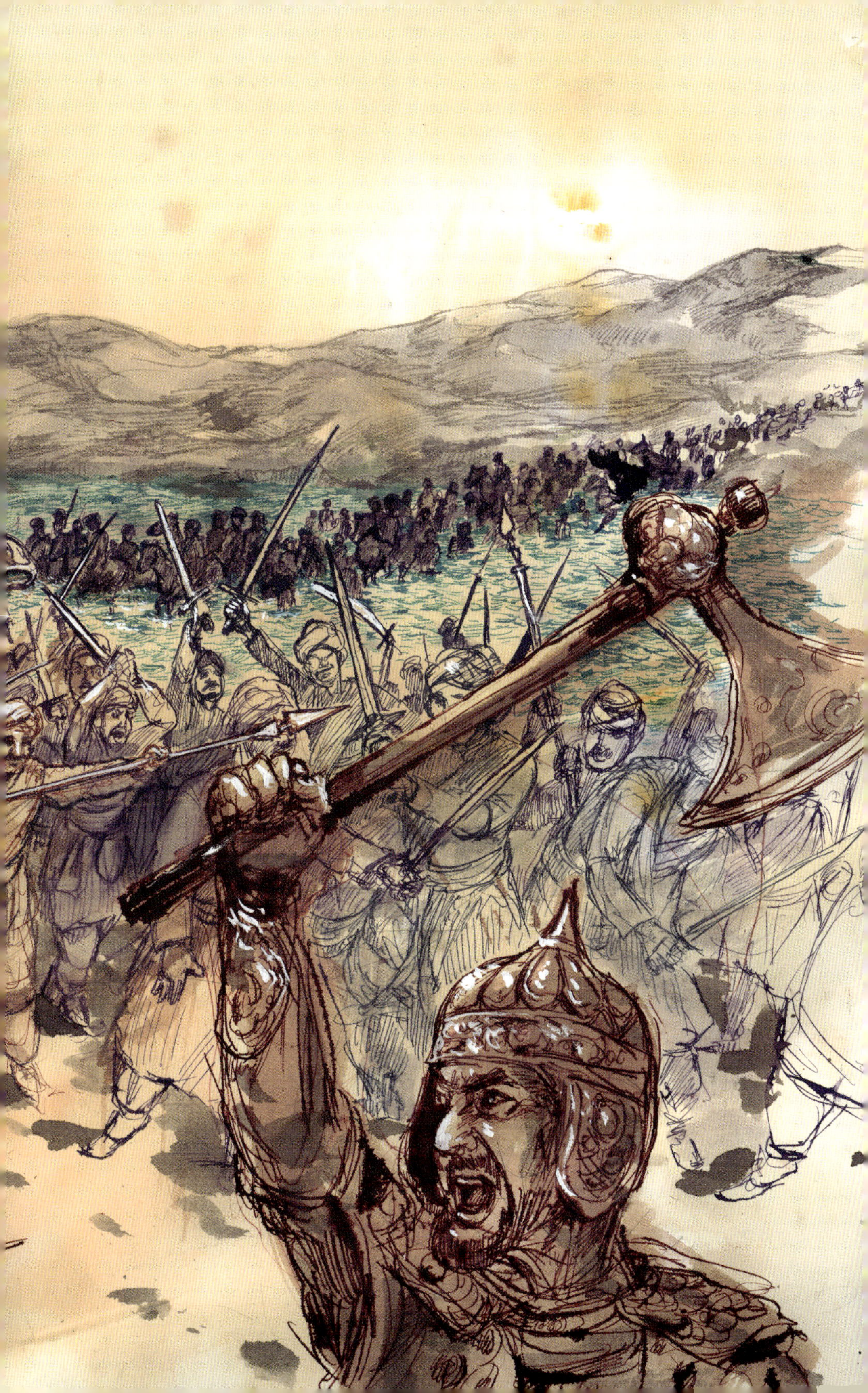

urged the injured animal back into the deepest part of the water. It managed to swim to the safety of their bank. As Nur retreated on the wounded elephant, a band of her followers assembled on the river's edge. They kept shooting to keep the enemy from coming after the empress. Many of those protecting her were slain.

Jahangir's master of ceremonies, a eunuch named Fidai Khan, led a group of soldiers across the river toward the emperor. They made it out of the water and as far as Shahryar's quarters, ringed by Mahabat's men. Fidai's horse was wounded, and four men fighting with him died. When it was clear that he couldn't break through to save the emperor, he raced back through the enemy line to the river, and swam to the other side.

The empress dismounted from her bleeding elephant and walked back to her brother's tent. Defeated, she understood that she would have to join her imprisoned husband on the other side of the river and accept—temporarily—Mahabat's terms. She vowed to come up with a new rescue plan. It would, she knew, take some time to formulate and execute. Her forces had suffered great losses. Scores of officers had been killed; high-ranking nobles had fled.

> The court poet Shirazi watched Nur bravely lead her men into battle. He wrote movingly of her courage in a long poem. In the part called "Chronicle of the Victory of Nur Jahan Begum," Shirazi said: "Her glory and dignity had captured the world."
>
> Paymaster historian Mutamad, fighting on Nur's side, wrote about the battle of 1626. So did Bhakkari. And two centuries later, a courtier named Muhammad Hadi wrote about it as well.

We do not know exactly when Nur returned to the side of the river where her husband was being held or whether she went willingly. Soon after her daring raid, the Mughal convoy moved on toward Kabul. Nur and Jahangir were at the center, but Mahabat was in charge of the halts, the marches, the order of procession. He kept up appearances. He was respectful to Jahangir. No one outside the cavalcade knew that the emperor and empress were captives.

When they reached Attock, they were still 240 miles southeast of Kabul. Mahabat asked permission from the emperor and empress to negotiate Asaf's surrender. Mahabat took Asaf into custody, promising to spare his life. He then ordered Asaf and his son to join the royals as captives on the road to Kabul. But he severely punished some of Asaf's men, executing many.

When Shah Jahan heard what Mahabat had done to his father, he flew into a rage. Partly because he feared an alliance between Mahabat and Parvez, and partly because he was eager to assure his father of his renewed allegiance, he decided to go after Mahabat. He set out from the south with a thousand horsemen, hoping to gather more support along the way. But one of his supporters died and his five-hundred-man cavalry unit disappeared. With only five hundred men left, Shah Jahan abandoned the idea of rescue and returned to the southern provinces.

Mahabat was, for the time being, at the helm of Mughal affairs. He told Jahangir, now a puppet emperor, what to do. He pushed Nur to the sidelines. Traveling as captives, the Mughals reached Kabul, nearly four hundred miles from the site of the kidnapping and the battle on the river. The residents gathered to greet them. The empress and emperor scattered coins as they moved through the marketplace. To the local people, this was an auspicious moment. They'd had no idea that the royal couple was in custody.

It was an unusual captivity. The two weren't held at gunpoint. Jahangir and Nur were prisoners, but their court and daily routines remained intact. Mahabat kept a close eye on the pair but let them visit the tombs of the emperor's great-grandfather and great-aunt. They went on an excursion to the garden near the Kabul fortress. They met with the leader of a local tribal people. Nur gave the leader's son gems and gilded utensils, gifts meant to forge a new alliance. The couple hunted ibexes, mountain rams, bears, and hyenas.

Nur Jahan maintained and regularly paraded her small cavalry. It was a ceremonial event that caused Mahabat no alarm.

A messenger brought news that Malik Ambar had died, but there was no longer any real Mughal military presence ready to take over the Deccan. A second piece of news was that Parvez had become seriously ill with an intestinal obstruction—the same malady that had allegedly killed his half-brother Khusraw. Gossip suggested that heavy drinking had contributed to Parvez's decline.

Behind the scenes, Nur Jahan was absorbed in planning the recovery of Mughal authority.

Her daily schedule allowed her to regularly meet with intimates and loyalists. With them, she began to quietly plan. To those warriors still in her troops, she promised that more reinforcements would come. She wooed resentful nobles back, holding out hopes of high offices and spending gold coins worth three hundred thousand rupees to build a network of support. She instructed her new eunuch to begin mustering troops in Lahore. He recruited two thousand horsemen and five thousand armed foot soldiers. All of this plotting took place in secret, unnoticed by the captor, while Jahangir pretended friendliness.

One day some of Mahabat's Rajput soldiers left their base camp and rode out to a well-known Kabul hunting ground to let their horses graze. This hunting preserve was in the care of royal guards called *ahadis*. An *ahadi* objected that the horses shouldn't be grazing in the preserve. The exchange turned nasty, and the Rajputs hacked him to pieces. When his relatives went to the court and cried out for justice, an official told them that the request would be forwarded to the emperor. Nur quietly sent out instructions to the *ahadis*, expert archers, explaining that they should move against Mahabat's men.

The next morning the *ahadis* attacked and killed nearly nine hundred Rajputs, several of them close associates of Mahabat's. He set out to help his men, but fearing that he might be killed in the fray, he changed his mind and returned to the safety of his compound. The attack shook him.

Following Nur's direction, the emperor tried to calm Mahabat. He showed Mahabat special favors. He took him into his confidence. The emperor even warned him that Nur intended to attack him, and that Asaf's daughter-in-law had said that whenever she had the opportunity, she would shoot Mahabat with a musket. As Jahangir gradually gained his captor's trust, Mahabat became less watchful. He trimmed the number of men stationed at the traveling palace compound. There were no further clashes, no disturbing incidents. But on the banks of the Bahat River, troops loyal to the empress were preparing for battle.

In early August 1626, the royal entourage left Kabul for the return trip to Lahore, still under the command of Mahabat. In a month's time, having covered nearly four hundred miles, they were near the spot where Mahabat had taken the emperor and empress captive. When the cavalcade was two days' ride from the Bahat River, Jahangir informed Mahabat that he wished to review Nur's cavalry. It would be best for Mahabat to postpone his own daily parade of troops, he said, lest words should pass between the two and lead to strife.

Mahabat saw this as another sign of collaboration on the part of the emperor. What he didn't know was that the empress had gathered her forces to confront him at the next stop on the journey to Lahore.

Jahangir sent a second communication, expressing his wish that Mahabat and his men move on in advance of the royal retinue to the Bahat River. Mahabat agreed, but he insisted that Asaf travel with him.

Instead of following Mahabat down the road, the royal retinue, including Nur's cavalry and nobles loyal to the emperor, took off at a brisk pace on a parallel route. They didn't stop for the night, and managed to cover two days' worth of traveling in one, reaching the river before Mahabat.

Nur, Jahangir, and their party crossed the river by boat. On the other side, Nur's cavalry was joined by the courtiers and soldiers she'd secretly gathered. Mahabat arrived. Quickly, he understood that Jahangir and Nur were now accompanied by a large number of troops loyal to them. The forces were enough to overpower him and his men. He knew that the imperial kidnapping was over. Nur had engineered the rescue of the emperor.

Mahabat was ordered to return Asaf and two nephews of Nur's who were still on the Kabul side of the river. In answer to Jahangir's order, Mahabat sent back one of the royal nephews. Regarding Asaf, he was candid in telling the messenger, "Since I have no assurance of my security from the begam [Nur], I fear that if I give Asaf Khan up, she will send an army down on me." Nur flew into a rage over these words. She sent the messenger back to Mahabat with a final order: "It is not in your best interests to delay in sending Asaf Khan, and do not allow yourself to think otherwise, for it will result in regret." Mahabat knew that Nur was a force to be reckoned with. He released Asaf immediately, holding on to one nephew as a safeguard. But he knew that his days of rising ambition and command were over. A few days later he sent the second nephew back to Nur.

Mahabat was banished to the eastern provinces, away from key centers of power and machinations. Jahangir exiled Mahabat rather than executing him for treason because Shah Jahan's behavior was even more concerning. Despite begging his father's forgiveness and sending his sons to Jahangir as a sign of fealty, Shah Jahan had renewed his rebellion. The emperor and empress feared that Mahabat and Shah Jahan might join hands. So they banished Mahabat to the outlying eastern provinces, far away from Shah Jahan.

Emperor Jahangir and the victorious Empress Nur Jahan returned to Lahore on October 18, 1626. The elite of the city lined the road to the palace. In a few weeks, the royal couple resumed the regular business of the court: administrative changes, new appointments, the shuffling of provincial governors. Jahangir appointed Asaf imperial deputy and governor of Punjab.

Nur's prominence in strategic and military planning caused much consternation. For many observers, the idea that Nur had fought Mahabat's men, suffered defeat, risen again, strategized, and rescued the emperor only proved that she had brought the Mughal world to chaos: *fitna*—as had happened centuries before when Ayisha fought the Battle of the Camel to try to protect the Prophet's line of succession. Only a few, like the poet Shirazi, recognized that Nur had preserved the Mughal order.

> *King Jahangir whose abode is exalted and elevated as the sky and who is King through the wise advice of the Queen....*
>
> *Never was witnessed in the region of my King such a fortified system (refuge) for the kingdom as the Queen.*

Twelve

THE LONG JOURNEY

According to a departure time set by the royal astrologers, the Mughal cavalcade left Lahore in March 1627 for the valley of Kashmir. As they had before, Nur and Jahangir endured the difficulties of the road to visit the delightful gardens of the north. The emperor would find relief from his escalating breathlessness and the empress could enjoy moments of leisure. Accompanying the royal retinue were Nur's brother Asaf, son-in-law Shahryar, and daughter, Ladli. Also in attendance was Prince Dawar Bakhsh, the son of the late blind Prince Khusraw. Dawar's popularity was growing among some Mughals. If there was even a small chance that he could block Shahryar's path to the throne, Nur wanted him where she could keep an eye on him.

Despite begging his father's forgiveness and sending him his sons as a sign of submission, Shah Jahan had renewed his rebellion. He was now fighting Mughal forces in the province of Sind. The Mughal commander—one of Nur's favored officers and Shahryar's former head of household—launched a cannon attack near the tent of once more pregnant Arjumand—a crime of "violating the imperial person" that Shah Jahan wouldn't forget. Then Shah Jahan himself fell ill.

While he was recovering at his camp, Nur sent him a message, explaining that harboring any imperial ambitions would be pointless. He had no backing, no men, no power. She was in charge. "It would be wisest to return to the Deccan and submit to your fate," she wrote. Shah Jahan did as she suggested. Soon after, Mahabat joined Shah Jahan. After the kidnapping fiasco, he'd realized that his only political option was casting his lot with Shah Jahan.

The air of Kashmir had lost its magic. Although it was frequently called "Paradise on earth" by the Mughals, Kashmir failed to restore Jahangir's vigor. His acute breathlessness troubled him; he suffered from severe chest pains and felt immensely weak. He couldn't even ride a horse and had to be carried in a palanquin. The royal physicians offered no hope of recovery.

In the months they were in Kashmir, Jahangir's conditioned worsened. He also developed an aversion to opium, a drug he had used for forty years. He lost his appetite and would take only a few bowls of grape wine each day. To Nur's alarm, he went in and out of lucidity, sometimes speaking gibberish.

With the emperor failing, Nur's son-in-law, Shahryar, gave her another cause for worry. The prince developed a case of Fox's disease, a kind of skin disorder, and was badly disfigured. He lost his hair, beard, eyebrows, and eyelashes. The royal physicians weren't able to help except to say that if Shahryar went back to warmer Lahore, he might recover. Early in October, Shahryar asked the empress for permission to travel, and she immediately agreed.

For Nur, the outlook was grim. Her husband was dying; the son-in-law she'd hoped would succeed him was threatened by disease.

Shahryar had barely left when Jahangir also decided to return to Lahore. Perhaps this was Nur's idea. She had good reason. It was imperative to have Shahryar close to the emperor as he breathed his last. The Mughals began the long return journey.

On the way, they stopped at Bahramgalla, a sweet green spot near a peak with a waterfall. Called White Water, it was a forceful cascade that foamed gloriously. For the first time in months, the emperor's condition improved a little. He said that he felt like hunting.

Preparations began at once. Servants set up a platform at the foot of the mountain, from which Jahangir could shoot with a musket. Soldiers would drive antelopes toward him. Once they were in sight, the emperor would aim his musket and fire. But as the hunt began, one of the soldiers lost his footing and plummeted to the ground and died. Jahangir was horrified. He summoned the soldier's grieving mother and paid her generous compensation. But his distress couldn't be lightened.

As the caravan advanced, the emperor deteriorated. Late in the day on October 28, as the party set out from the town of Rajouri, he called for wine. His attendants brought him a cup, but he was unable to swallow. By the time they reached the imperial resting house at Chingiz Hatli, the emperor's breathing was ragged.

> Yes, he had taken a vow not to hunt. But at this point when he was dying, everything he wished for seemed reasonable to those around him.

Jahangir loved this resting house's stone walls, carved with floral patterns, and its fine terrace. Now the brick gateway, shielded with weeping grass, gave passage to an emperor clearly failing. The empress, her brother, important nobles, physicians, and servants gathered around him.

At dawn on October 29, 1627, as the light changed, Jahangir died. He was fifty-eight.

Mughal chroniclers have different points of view about what happened immediately after Jahangir's death. Bhakkari says that Nur Jahan, determined to promote Shahryar as successor, wanted to arrest her brother Asaf, who favored his son-in-law Shah Jahan. No other court historian mentions this. The imperial history commissioned by Shah Jahan many years later says that in the aftermath of Jahangir's death, Nur was "scheming to install her son-in-law Shahryar on the throne." Most accounts agree that in the Mughal camp, still more than a hundred miles from Lahore, the battle for succession began at once. Nur summoned key nobles to a conference, but no one showed up. Asaf, usually discreet and diplomatic, had promptly taken charge and preempted his sister's command. He came out forcefully in support of his son-in-law Shah Jahan. Asaf sent a swift messenger to deliver the news of Jahangir's death to Shah Jahan.

The problem for Asaf was how to hold the Mughal throne until Shah Jahan arrived from the south. He summoned Jahangir's grandson Dawar Bakhsh and promised him that he would be the next king. Although Dawar was a pawn in Asaf's plot, a placeholder, he agreed to the offer of the throne after Asaf took an oath of loyalty to him.

When Nur found out about Asaf's plans for Dawar, she was dumbstruck. Then panic-stricken.

Nur Jahan mourned her husband and feared for her position. She sent messenger after messenger summoning her brother to meet her. Asaf made excuses and never showed up.

He isolated her and sent away her officers, companions, and supporters. Bhakkari wrote of Nur's predicament, "You shall be treated as you have treated."

Within days of the emperor's death, all the men who had bowed before Nur had deserted her. Almost unanimously, the nobles in the camp endorsed Asaf's strategy of putting Dawar on the throne in order to secure the accession of Shah Jahan. With her husband gone and her brother opposing her, none of Nur's maneuvers was likely to succeed. At a rather astonishing speed, the old order was restored. It was as if these men had simply been waiting for the emperor's passing so that they could override the empress.

Under the watchful eye of her brother, Nur prepared to send the emperor's body to Lahore to bury him with full imperial honors. The procession split into three groups. The first carried Jahangir's body, escorted by servants and attendants. The second included Asaf, Dawar, and important nobles and dignitaries. Third, far out in the procession line, a day's ride behind the others, was Nur. She followed at quite a distance behind her husband's body, riding an elephant. Asaf had carefully chosen the servants now attending her, but Nur managed to make sure that the three sons of Shah Jahan in the Mughal party rode with her. The princes ensured Nur's safety.

> Shah Jahan had earlier sent two of his sons to Jahangir as a sign of submission. Shuja, the epileptic prince, had been in the care of the empress.

Along the way, funeral rites were performed for the late emperor, including a last wash of the royal body. The removal of the entrails was meant to save the corpse from early decomposition. A man's closest male relatives usually tended to these rites. Asaf and Dawar likely supervised. In this way the royal body was prepared for burial, which would take place, as the emperor had wished, in the Heart-Contenting Garden in Shahdara, just outside Lahore; Nur had designed it.

Meanwhile, a mullah officially but not very publicly proclaimed Dawar the Mughal king.

※

In Lahore, as soon as Shahryar got the news of his father's death, he raided the treasury and took goods from the imperial workshops. He distributed these riches to win supporters. He gathered troops and seized the departments within easy reach — those dealing with elephants, the stables, and the armory.

Thinking of her mother's safety, Ladli urged Shahryar to take charge of the empire. To further cement his support, he gave large amounts of money to numerous officers and nobles. He promised money and royal appointments to others. A cousin took command of his forces.

The procession reached Lahore a few weeks after the emperor's death. Soon thereafter, the emperor was buried in Shahdara, near Lahore. The burial rites were barely over when Asaf and the puppet king Dawar started a battle with Shahryar's men on the outskirts of Lahore. Mounted on elephants, Asaf and Dawar fought alongside other seasoned nobles. Shahryar himself remained in the Lahore fort, clearly fearful. His undisciplined troops soon scattered in all directions. Asaf and the imperial army then entered the fort. Most of Shahryar's men deserted him and joined Asaf's camp. Shahryar hid in a corner of his late father's harem.

A trusted eunuch brought Shahryar out of the harem, his hands bound with the sash from his waist, and led him to Dawar. The puppet king sat on the throne inside the citadel of Lahore, surrounded by courtiers under the control of Asaf. When Shahryar's hands were released, he offered the puppet emperor *taslim*, placing the back of his right hand on the ground, raising it gently as he stood erect, and setting the palm of his hand upon the crown of his head. But the obeisance did Shahryar no good. At Asaf's orders, imperial guards imprisoned the prince in an isolated section of the fort. Two days later he was blinded.

Asaf sent a second message to Shah Jahan, begging him to proceed to Lahore "on wings of haste." Asaf feared that a shake-up was still possible while Nur was near. She almost certainly would have prolonged the struggle for the Mughal throne if she could have, but there was nothing left to do. With all the leading nobles and military leaders in her brother's camp, she was no longer free to act. She wasn't at the Lahore fort. She was held as a prisoner in Shahdara, where she would soon build the tomb of her late husband. Records don't say where Ladli or her daughter were at this point.

After four days of mourning and consultations with astrologers, Shah Jahan set out for Agra, which he intended to make his permanent capital. When he received Asaf's second message urging him to hurry, he sent a reply ordering Asaf to execute his half-brother Shahryar, the puppet king Dawar, and the cousin who'd supported Shahryar. While Shah Jahan was still en route, Asaf had a mullah declare Shah Jahan the new Mughal king. That way, Asaf ensured that the prince would be legally recognized as king by all in power. Dawar, the king with the shortest reign in Mughal history—less than a month—was arrested. He, Shahryar, and everyone on Shah Jahan's list were executed—including Nur's loyalist who had shot a cannon near the tent of his favorite wife. Thus, Shah Jahan marched north in a triumphal procession. Along the way, regional landlords and grandees professed their loyalty. In return, he promised new appointments and future honors.

On February 3, 1628, the day of his formal accession to the throne, Shah Jahan mounted an elephant and rode through Agra scattering heaps of coins to his right and left. He entered the fort and sat upon the throne in the Hall of Public Audience. Almost immediately, he ordered the treasury to strike coins bearing his name as new emperor of Mughal India.

The new emperor rewarded his supporters handsomely. His father-in-law Asaf, the central player in ensuring his accession to the throne, received the highest rank. Asaf became the *wakil*, the highest minister, and he got the governorships of Lahore and Multan. And more: he was honored as "Right Hand of the State," and he was put in charge of the special imperial seal. Mahabat became the commander-in-chief of the army.

In the absence of a man in whose name she could fight, and with no nobles or family members supporting or celebrating her imperial service, Nur could take no further action to retain her position as co-sovereign. Her rise to power had been swift, but her fall was even swifter.

The official historians of Shah Jahan's reign deliberately wrote Nur's merits and accomplishments out of Mughal history. Her extraordinary achievements were omitted: the emperor's twentieth wife, not from a Mughal family, who became co-sovereign, the only woman ruler in Mughal India; the commander of a battle on a roaring river who rescued a kidnapped emperor; the accomplished huntress and tiger slayer; the compassionate ruler of the court and harem who transformed the lives of orphan girls with the marriages she arranged.

When Nur wasn't made absent from the histories, she was blamed for the chaos that befell the empire. Shah Jahan attempted to erase Nur from history in another way: he revoked the coins bearing Nur's and Jahangir's images to wipe out all memory of her power. But collecting the coins already in circulation would have been extraordinarily difficult, and Nur's coins survive to this day in museums.

The erasure of Nur Jahan's contributions and accomplishments extended even to her husband's tomb. The basic facts about its construction and patronage were hotly contested in the histories from Shah Jahan's time, as well as in the public square. In 1660, the writer Muhammad Salih Kanbo described Jahangir's tomb as Shah Jahan's project. The only concession Kanbo made to Nur Jahan's involvement was to say that the Heart-Contenting Garden around the tomb had belonged to the empress. It was a pleasure garden she had designed and which she'd frequently visited with Jahangir.

Architecture experts and historians, however, are clear about the fact that Jahangir's tomb was the product of Nur Jahan's vision. Soon after his father's death, Shah Jahan gave the orders for its construction. But the tomb was designed by and built under the supervision of Nur Jahan.

Nur Jahan lived for another eighteen years. She chose not to stay in the harem of her stepson, as other elder Mughal women had done. If she had, Asaf and Shah Jahan would eventually have turned to her for counsel, as kings and nobles had with other matriarchs for generations. She chose a life of independence, spent in a mansion outside Lahore. Legends say that Ladli and her granddaughter lived with her. She received members of royal family and perhaps even guided the younger princesses, such as her grandniece Jahanara. The daughter of Arjumand and Shah Jahan, Jahanara was born in 1614 while her father, then known as Prince Khurram, was on a campaign against Mewar. On the road and in court, she could closely observe the activities of Empress Nur, taking them in even if she didn't fully understand their import. Coming of age when her great-aunt Nur was at the height of her powers, Jahanara would have seen the empress personally supervising the care of her younger brother Prince Shuja, discussing family matters with her mother, Arjumand, designing buildings, making key political decisions.

Nur's resources as empress and an aristocratic landowner had been sizable. An eighteenth-century biographer of Mughal nobles estimated that her estates alone were worth more than her father's. By law, she would retain these property rights until her death, when they would be returned to the imperial exchequer. The records of the British East India Company and other European traders and visitors in India tell us that she also accrued a great deal of profit in commerce.

The aging Nur was resourceful and experienced. As she had done so many times before, she rolled up her sleeves and went about her business. As before, she spent lavishly on the poor and needy.

And, as we know, she supervised and designed a splendid tomb in her husband's memory. It took her ten years, from 1628 to 1638, to complete this monument. Jahangir wanted a tomb that allowed direct connection with the divine. That would translate to designing an uncovered tomb. There was no model for it. Nur devised a monumental open platform. It had high minarets at the four corners, open to the sky, the rain, and the clouds, ready to receive divine mercy. She would repeat the same style for her own tomb, which she designed herself.

Nur passed away on November 18, 1645. Even the official history of Shah Jahan's reign, which erased Nur's contributions and accomplishments, acknowledged her greatness:

> *In the city of Lahore, the Queen Dowager Nur Jahan Begam—whom it is needless to praise as she had already reached the pinnacle of fame—departed to Paradise in the seventy-second year of her age. . . . From the sixth year of the late Emperor's reign, when she was united to him in the bond of matrimony, she gradually acquired such unbounded influence over His Majesty's mind that she seized the reins of government and abrogated to herself the supreme civil and financial administration of the realm, ruling with absolute authority till the conclusion of his reign.*

The remarkable Nur Jahan and her influence come into view undiluted despite the disparaging tone of Shah Jahan's chronicle.

In the centuries that followed, a cartoonish image of a besotted Emperor Jahangir came to dominate the public imagination as the most likely explanation of Nur's power. She rose because of her husband's excessive drinking and indulgent nature, it was said. She rose because he was besotted by her. *Jahangir and Nur Jahan met in the Meena Bazaar. He fell in love with her. They married.* Popular works about the empress focused strongly on this imperial love story. Nur's birth on the road became the favorite opening scene of films, plays, and novels about her. Most of them revel in her use of feminine wiles to gain influence in the harem and the court. Nearly all of them end at Nur's marriage in 1611. The emphasis on her romance with Jahangir truncated her biography in a way that diminished her. In the popular imagination, Nur's story stopped at the very moment when her life's best work began.

Nur's history tells us so much more about her life and work. She certainly embodied love. It was a capacious kind of love: for orphan girls, for the people she saved from a killer tiger, for her employees, and for her kith and kin. She was wise, and intentional, and we see her decisive in thought and action as she directs her courtiers to save Jahangir from captivity. Her power and resilience were visible to family members, court historians, poets, and diplomats. Her brilliant strategy shines, especially in her rescue of Jahangir. The signs of her leadership and beauty were also there in her gifts, coins, and monuments. The extraordinary story of Nur Jahan is dynamic. She comes into view, above all, as a humane, magnificent empress.

Acknowledgments

On a bitterly cold December night in 2016, I was enjoying an evening with my two nieces, then ages ten and fourteen. The winter chill in Delhi can pierce, and when the temperature outside plummets, the indoors in most homes is no different if you don't have electric heaters. I was in India on an annual family and research trip that winter and could not wait to crank up the heaters and visit with my nieces in the cozy sitting room of my sister's apartment.

I was then working on the opening scene of my book *Empress: The Astonishing Reign of Nur Jahan*.

I had told my nieces occasional stories of Nur Jahan, the magnificent sixteenth-century empress of India, just as my mother had done for me in my girlhood. My nieces knew that Nur was born on the road outside a fort town in Afghanistan and that she grew up in north India and spoke many languages. They knew that Nur became the Great Mughal emperor's twentieth wife — and eventually rose to be the only woman co-ruler among the Great Mughals.

When I finished the extraordinary tale of how Nur saved the village from the killer tiger by shooting it from atop an enormous elephant, the girls released a torrent of questions: What was she wearing? Where did she learn to shoot? Would she teach her daughter to shoot? I told more Nur stories, and they grew more

ACKNOWLEDGMENTS

excited. "Why don't you write this book for us," one of them said. "And you can have so many pictures, of the tiger, the elephant."

I listened, smiling at their wonderful curiosity. After *Empress* was released, in July 2018, I began traveling to national and international venues for discussions, presentations, and talks to help promote the book. During several of those events, people asked me whether I'd write *Empress* for young adults.

At the Jaipur Literary Festival in Boulder, I was preparing for an interview. With twenty minutes to kill before my session, I walked into the greenroom; a few minutes later a woman joined me there. "Hi, I am Molly Crabapple," she said. "Lovely to meet you, what a fine book," I replied, referring to *Brothers of the Gun*, which she and Marwan Hisham had launched that morning. "I am Ruby Lal." "*Empress*!" she exclaimed. We met again in India, in Lebanon, and in New York.

And then came the pandemic. In October 2020, I was in Uppsala, Sweden, on a fellowship. Molly and I were writing letters to each other: she sent me her art via letters, and I sent her stories of my Scandinavian life. At a talk there, someone asked, "Why not a YA *Empress*?" Two weeks later, on two successive Zoom interviews, I heard that question yet again: Why not? And then it clicked: I knew that I was waiting for a co-creator. Molly and I chatted across the seas and cooked up a plan for a remix of *Empress*.

Warm thanks to my nieces Aashna and Ananya for first planting the idea of a YA book. Even though she was not in Delhi on that evening, my niece Fanny loved the plan. Bridget Matzie, my agent, has a liking for big topics. I am thrilled that she found *Tiger Slayer* appealing. To Molly: I am grateful for our long, probing conversations on art. Playing with art and form were the best

154

preoccupations of my days as I wrote this book. Much gratitude to Simon Boughton for his sensitive care with words and stories, for insights and fine edits. Special thanks to Bahar Beihaghi, who posed as Nur; to Murtaza Hussain, as Jahangir; and to everyone who spent an afternoon modeling as a Mughal for Molly to paint. And finally, thanks to Jason Reynolds for his writings.

          Ruby Lal
          Atlanta, Georgia
          January 2025

Sources and Notes

This work is based on my book *Empress: The Astonishing Reign of Nur Jahan* (Norton, 2018). An exhaustive bibliography can be found in *Empress* and includes all the court-related sources cited here, as well as other Persian records, legends, scholarly and reader-friendly books, and references to paintings that are key to the life and times of the Mughal empress Nur Jahan. For discussions of Nur Jahan, a reader-friendly English translation of the memoirs of her husband, Jahangir, is by W. M. Thackston: *The Jahangirnama: Memoirs of Jahangir, Emperor of India* (New York: Oxford University Press, 1999). Readers might enjoy the fascinating journals of Sir Thomas Roe, James I's ambassador to the Mughal court: Sir William Foster, ed., *The Embassy of Sir Thomas Roe to India*, 1615–19 (New Delhi: Munshiram Manoharlal Publishers, 1990; first Indian ed.). For Mughal architecture of Akbar and his capital city, see Michael Brand and Glenn D. Lowry, *Akbar's India: Art from the Mughal City of Victory* (New York: Asia Society Galleries, 1986). For a bibliographic work on art, see Milo C. Beach, Eberhard Fischer, and B. N. Goswamy, eds., *Masters of Indian Painting* (Artibus Asiae Publishers, 2011). For a feminist history of the itinerant Mughal court, feminine experiences, and harem life, see Ruby Lal, *Vagabond Princess: The Great Adventures of Gulbadan* (New Haven and London: Yale University Press, 2024).

Abul Hasan's portrait of Nur Jahan holding a musket (Chapter Seven) can be viewed together with other contemporary images

SOURCES AND NOTES

of Nur and her world at my website, https://rubylal.com/empress-photo-gallery/ and among the photos included in my book *Empress: The Astonishing Reign of Nur Jahan*.

Sources of direct quotations are cited as follows.

CHAPTER 2:
CARAVAN NURSERY AND BEYOND

14 **"all the Indian parrots"**: Muzaffar Alam, *The Languages of Political Islam in India, c. 1200–1800* (New Delhi: Permanent Black, 2004), 123.

CHAPTER 3:
THE MIRROR OF HAPPINESS

22 *They should not be allowed to read or write*: G. M. Wickens, trans. and ed., *The Nasirean Ethics* (London: George Allen and Unwin, 1964), 173.

CHAPTER 5:
LIGHT OF THE PALACE TO LIGHT OF THE WORLD

48 **"boundless and unlimited"**: Farid Bhakkari, *Nobility Under the Great Mughals: Based on Dhakhiratul Khawanin of Shaikh Farid Bhakkari*, Parts 1–3, trans. Z. A. Desai (New Delhi: Sundeep Prakashan, 2003), 15.

49 **"strength of her personality"**: Bhakkari, *Dhakhiratul Khawanin*, 15.

50 **"She has considered it a pleasure"**: Alexander Rogers and Henry Beveridge, eds., *Tuzuk-i Jahangiri or Memoirs of Jahangir*, 2 vols. (London: Royal Asiatic Society, 1909), 2:214–15; hereafter cited as *Tuzuk*.

50 **"seized with fever . . . was fonder of me"**: *Tuzuk*, 1:266–67.

57 **"If one drop"**: *Tuzuk*, 1:270–71.

SOURCES AND NOTES

57 *If the rosebud*: Muhammad Hashim Khafi Khan, *Muntakhab-ul-Lubab*, ed. Kabiruddin Ahmad, 2 vols. (Calcutta: Bibliotheca Indica, Asiatic Society of Bengal, 1869), 1:270–71.

59 "I ordered Nur-mahall Begam": *Tuzuk*, 1:318–19.

64 "Until now, such shooting": *Tuzuk*, 1:375 and 375n1.

64 *Though Nur Jahan be in form a woman*: *Tuzuk*, 1:375 and 375n1.

CHAPTER 6:
NUR BECOMES CO-SOVEREIGN

68 "Such offerings had never been made": *Tuzuk*, 1:401; S. A. I. Tirmizi, *Edicts from the Mughal Harem* (1979; repr., New Delhi: Idarah-I Adabiyat-I Delli, 2009), xi.

70 "more than a thowsand" women: William Foster, ed., *The Embassy of Sir Thomas Roe to India, 1615–19* (Delhi: Munshiram Manoharlal Publishers, 1990; 1st Indian ed.), 270.

72 "and listen[ed] to her dictates": Mu'tamad Khan, *The Iqbalnama-i Jahangiri* (Calcutta: Asiatic Society of Bengal, 1865), 405.

CHAPTER 7:
PORTRAIT FOR AN EMPRESS

75 "fifteen hundred thousand": Jos Gommans, *Mughal Warfare: Indian Frontiers and High Roads to Empire, 1500–1700* (London: Routledge, 2003), 99.

77 "An elephant is not at ease": *Tuzuk*, 2:104–5.

CHAPTER 8:
DELAYED HONEYMOON

85 "Was there any king": *Intekhab-i Jahangir Shahi*, B.M. Or. 1648, folios 320–22.

SOURCES AND NOTES

88 **"The flowers of Kashmir"**: *Tuzuk*, 2:134.
90 ***There is a ruby button***: Muhammad Hashim Khafi Khan, *Muntakhab-ul-Lubab*, 1:270.
90 **"fish so tame"**: François Bernier, *Travels in the Mogul Empire, A.D. 1656–1668*, ed. and trans. Archibald Constable (1916; repr., New Delhi: S. Chand, 1968), 413n2, 414.

CHAPTER 9:
BABY TAJ

101 **"That ungrateful man"**: *Tuzuk*, 2: 212–14.
102 **"greater than those of the physicians"**: *Tuzuk*, 2:214.
102 **"What can one write?"**: *Tuzuk*, 2:216–17.
103 **"Do you recognize him?"**: *Tuzuk*, 2:222.

CHAPTER 10:
ANARCHY

109 **"Of which of my pains"**: W. M. Thackston, *The Jahangirnama: Memoirs of Jahangir, Emperor of India* (New York: Oxford University Press, 1999), 387.
109 **She "changed everything"**: Bhakkari, *Dhakhiratul Khawanin*, 20.
113 **"Is that what the Messenger of God ordered"**: Fatima Mernissi, *The Forgotten Queens of Islam* (Minneapolis: University of Minnesota Press, 1993), 66–67.
117 **what sounded like a thousand cannon balls:** Thackston, *Jahangirnama*, 425–27; citations on 426.

CHAPTER 11:
A DARING RAID

124 **"You have been disgraced"**: Thackston, *Jahangirnama*, 441.

SOURCES AND NOTES

124 **"Without her the flower"**: *Fathnama-i Nur Jahan Begum*, Center for Advanced Study Library, Aligarh Muslim University, Rotograph 10, 132.

124 **"source of deceit and deception"**: *Fathnama-i Nur Jahan Begum*, 132, 134, 136.

125 **"Her Majesty wants to know"**: Thackston, *Jahangirnama*, 442.

128 **"Her glory and dignity"**: *Fathnama-i Nur Jahan Begum*, 148.

134 **"Since I have no assurance"**: Thackston, *Jahangirnama*, 447.

134 **"It is not in your best interests"**: Thackston, *Jahangirnama*, 447.

135 ***King Jahangir whose abode***: *Fathnama-i Nur Jahan Begum*, 256.

CHAPTER 12:
THE LONG JOURNEY

137 **"violating the imperial person"**: Munis D. Faruqui, *The Princes of the Mughal Empire, 1504–1719* (Cambridge: Cambridge University Press, 2012), 254.

137 **"It would be wisest to return"**: Thackston, *Jahangirnama*, 450.

140 **"scheming to install"**: W. E. Begley and Z. A. Desai, eds. and comps., *The Shah Jahan Nama of 'Inayat Khan* (Delhi: Oxford University Press, 1990), 12.

141 **"You shall be treated"**: Bhakkari, *Dhakhiratul Khawanin*, 21.

143 **"on wings of haste"**: Thackston, *Jahangirnama*, 458.

148 *"In the city of Lahore, the Queen Dowager"*: Begley and Desai, *Shah Jahan Nama*, 333–34.

Index

Page numbers in italic refer to illustrations.

Abul Fazl, 37
Abul-Hasan, 78–82, *80*
Agra, 14, *24–25*
    Fort of, 38–40
    Mihr's family's move to, 23–24
    Shah Jahan's march to, 111–12, 144
ahadis, 131
Akbar, xiii
    Asmat's uncle employed by, 14
    court of, 4
    death of, 36
    Ghiyas's first meeting with, 16–18, *17*
    Great Comet, 1–2
    history commissioned by, 37
    Mughal Empire under, *xiv–xv*
    names for, 15
    stories favored by, 25
Akbarnama, 37
Alexander the Great, 19
Al-Hind, 2; *See also* India

Ali, Ayisha's battle against, 113
Ali Quli Beg, xiii
    background of, 30
    death of, 39
    Mihr's marriage with, 27–31, *28–29*, *31–35*
    Salim/Jahangir disliked by, 37–38
    as Slayer of Tigers, 34
Allahabad, 115
Aqa Reza, 79
Arjumand (Mumtaz Mahal; Exalted One of the Palace)
    daughter of, 146–47
    as influential adviser, 49–50
    at Ladli's wedding ceremonies, 98
    marriage of, 45, 92
    during Shah Jahan's revolt, 115
    at Sind battle, 137
    Taj Mahal tribute to, 100
Asaf Khan, xiii, 20, *110*
    in battle for Jahangir's successor, 140–41, 143–44

INDEX

Asaf Khan (*continued*)
   as influential adviser, 49
   during Jahangir's kidnapping, 119, 121–25
   in Ladli's marriage ceremonies, 95, 98
   in Mahabat's defeat, 132, 134
   in Mihr's marriage to Jahangir, 45, 47
   as Punjab governor, 135
   on return following kidnapping of Jahangir, 136
   Salim as model for, 26
   Shah Jahan's rewards to, 145
   Shah Jahan supported by, 95–96, 110–11, 140
   surrender of, 129
Asmat Begum, xiii, 2–3
   background, 2, 6
   birth of Mihr, 8, 10, 11
   in caravan from Persia to India, 2–8, 12
   in caravan in India, 12–14
   death of, 102
   harem visit, 41
   as influential adviser, 49
   at Ladli's wedding ceremonies, 98
   in Lahore, 13, 14
   at Mihr's wedding, 27
   parenting, 23
   in the Red City, 14, 15
   scent made by, 57
   tomb designed for, *104–5*, 105–6
   visit to palace quarters by, 26–27
Ayisha, 113, 135

Babur, 106
"Baby Taj" (garden tomb), *104–5*, 105–6
Bahat River, 86–88, *86–88*
   Jahangir's kidnapping near, 118, *119*, 124–25, 128
   Nur's defeat of Mahabat at, 132–34, *135*
Bahramgalla, 139
balcony appearances, 72, *73*
Banaras, 115
Baramula, 86
Baroman, 70
Battle of the Camel, 113, 135
bazaars
   imperial, Nur's presence in, 66
   portable Mughal bazaars, 69–70
Bengal, 31–35, 115
Bengali language, 34, 35
Bernier, François, 90–91
Bhuliyas, 87
Bhuliyas Pass, 87
Bihar, 115

INDEX

boys
  education for, 21–23
  within nobles' homes, 20
  separation of girls and, 26
Brahmins, 103
Burdwan, 31, 32

Camp of Good Fortune, *53–55*, 53–60, 65
caravan(s), 5–14, *6–7*; *See also* travel
ceremonies; *See also* weddings
  imperial, Nur's presence in, 61, 66
  in teaching, 21
  weighing of the emperor, 50, 102
Chingiz Hatli, 139
Christianity, 3, 10
clothing
  in Burdwan, 33, 34
  given to the needy, 21
  for Mihr's wedding, 27
  for nobles, 6
  Nur Mahali, 49, *49*
  Nur's design of wedding dresses, 48
coins, 71–72, 145, 146
comets, 1, 5, 8
court culture, Mughal, 92

Dai, 7; *See also* Dilaram/Dai Dilaram
Dal Lake, *89*, 89–90

Damodar river, 32
Dawar Bakhsh, xiii
  battle for the throne, 140–44
  execution of, 144
  as king, 142–44
  on return following kidnapping, 136
Deccan
  battles for, 57, 58, 84, 92, 103, 107–9, 111
  Mughal takeover of, 130
  Shah Jahan's retreat toward, 117
Delhi, 14, 83, 114
designs by Nur
  garden tomb, *104–5*, 105–6
  Heart-Contenting Garden, 142
  inn, 78–79, *79*
  Jahangir's tomb, 146, 147
  Nur's own tomb, 147
  wedding dresses for poor brides, 48
Dilaram/Dai Dilaram, xiii
  as family head of staff, 23, 24
  as head of harem, 83
  as influential adviser, 49
  on journey from Persia, 6, 7
  on journey to Agra, 39
  and Ladli's birth, 34
  at Ladli's wedding ceremonies, 98
  at Mihr's wedding, 27
  move to Burdwan with Mihr, 31–32

INDEX

Dow, Alexander, 11
Dulac, Edmund, x, xi
Durga, 34

education, 21–23, *22*, 35
Eid, 25
eunuchs, 119, 120

Farid Bhakkari, 48, 110, 128, 140
Fatehpur-Sikri (Red City), 14–18, *15*
feasts
   Eid, 24, 25
   at Ramsar, 60, 66
   at wedding, 100
festivals
   kinds of, 24, 25
   seasonal, 66
   in teaching culture, 21
Fidai Khan, 128
fitna (civil strife), 112–13
foods
   in Bengal, 34, 35
   given to the needy, 21
   in Lahore, 13–14
   table attendants for tasting, 30
funeral rites, 141, 142

Ganesha, 34
garden tomb ("Baby Taj"), *104–5*, *105–6*

gender divisions, 3
   in authority and sovereignty, 70–72
   in education, 21–23
   within nobles' homes, 20
Ghiyas Beg, xiii, 2–3
   on Asmat's death, 102
   background of, 2, 6
   during birth of Mihr, 8, 10, 11
   calligraphy of, 22
   in caravan from Persia to India, 2–8, 12
   in caravan through India, 12–14
   death of, 103
   descendants of married to emperors, 97
   first meeting of Akbar and, 16–18, *17*
   in imperial government, 18
   as influential adviser, 49
   Jahangir's promotions of, 45, 47
   as Jahangir's trusted advisor, 38–39
   at Ladli's betrothal to Shahryar, 93
   at Ladli's wedding ceremonies, 98, 100
   in Lahore, 13, 14
   Nur's inheritance from, 103–4
   parenting by, 23
   tomb designed for, *104–5*, *105–6*

INDEX

girls
    education for, 21–23
    in harems, 41–42; *See also* harems
    within nobles' homes, 20
    separation of boys and, 26
Great Comet, 1–2, 5, 8

Hafiz, 14, 23
Haidar Malik, 90
Hardwar, 102–3
harem, 41, *44*
    during battle, 115
    Mihr and Ladli in, 40–45
    Nur's influence in, 48–50
Hari Parbat, 89, *89*
Harkha, xiii
    as harem matriarch, 45
    at Ladli's wedding ceremonies, 96–98
    on trip to Kashmir, 74
Heart-Contenting Garden, 142, 146
Himalayas, 84–89
Hindavi, 14, 21, 34, 35
Hinduism, 21, 61, 66, 103
history(-ies)
    accounts of Nur in, 140, 145–46, 148–49
    of Mughal Empire, 37, 140
    sources, 10–11
History of Jahangir, The, 10

holiday celebrations, 66; *See also* feasts
houses, 20, 33, *34*
hunting
    Jahangir's last hunt, 139
    Kabul hunting preserve, 131
    by Nur, 61–64, *63*, 75–78, *76*, *77*
    in Srinagar, 90

India
    caravan in, 12–14
    Mihr's birth on way to, 2–11
    Mihr's family arrival in, 12–14
    nobles' homes open to visitors, 12–13
    wealth of, 4
Iran, 2; *See also* Persia
Islam, 3
    Battle of the Camel, 113, 135
    Mihr's study of, 34
    Muslim festivals, 24–25
I'timad ud-Daula's (Pillar of the State) Tomb, *104–5*, 105–6

Jadrup, 61–62, 83
Jahanara, 146–47
Jahangir (Conqueror of the World), xiii, 36; *See also* Salim
    alcohol and drug use by, 50–51
    burial of, 143

INDEX

Jahangir (Conqueror of the World) (*continued*)
   co-sovereign with Nur, 57, 60–61, 65–73, 113
   death of, 139
   during defeat of Mahabat, 131–35
   delayed honeymoon with Nur, 83–92
   expansion of territories by, 57, 58
   as fourth Mughal emperor, 36, 38
   funeral rites for, 141–42
   Ghiyas's property given to Nur by, 103–4
   harem of, 40–45, *44*
   Hasan's paintings of, 80
   health of, 92–93, 101–2, 109, 137–39, *138*
   historical image of, 148, 149
   history written by, 10
   Jadrup visited by, 83
   Khusraw's rebellion against, 38–39
   Mahabat's disputes with, 120–22
   Mahabat's kidnapping of, 118–20, 122–32, *126–27*
   and marriage of Shahryar and Ladli, 97
   Mihr renamed by, 47, 59
   Mihr's wedding to, 45–47, *46–47*
   mobile court of, 52–60, *53–55*
   names given to women by, 59
   on Nur's hunting skill, 64
   Nur's relationship with, 49, 50
   and Quli's death, 39
   reconciliation of Khusraw and, 75
   Shah Jahan's rebellion against, 107–17
   tomb of, 146, 147
   trip to Kashmir by, 74–78
   visit to Jadrup by, 61–62
Jahangir and Prince Khurram Feasted by Nur Jahan, 68
Jalandhar, 78
Jawahir Khan, 119
Judaism, 3

Kabul, 130, 131
Kali, 34
Kandahar, 5, 107–13
Kangra, 103
Kashmir, 137
   Bernier on, 90–91, *91*
   flowers of, 88
   Nur and Jahangir's trips to, 74–78, 136
Khafi Khan, 11
Khurram (joyous), xiii, 43, *43*
   at Camp of Good Fortune, 54, 55
   Deccan campaign of, 57, 58, 65–66
   gifts to Nur from, 68

INDEX

in harem quarters, 42
as influential adviser, 50
marriage of Arjumand and, 45
Nur's gifts to, 54–56, *56*, 66–67, *67*
Nur's support of, 51
title bestowed on, 66; *See also* Shah Jahan

Khusraw, xiii, 43, *43*
death of, 107
illness of, 103
rebellion against Jahangir by, 38–39
on second operation in Deccan, 84
trip to Kashmir by, 75

Krishna, 34, 75

Ladli (beloved; the loved one), xiii
birth of, 34
childhood of, 34–35
in Jahangir's harem, 40–41, 44
Nur's choice of husband for, 91–94
wedding of Shahryar and, 93–100, *96–97*, *99*

Lahore, 13–14, 92
Jahangir and Nur's return to, 135, 138–39
Jahangir's funeral in, 143
Mahabat's kidnapping of Jahangir in, 121–23
Mahabat's return to, 132

Mihr's family's arrival in, 12, 13
languages, 14, 21, 34, 35
Light-Scattering Garden, 100

Mahabat Khan, xiii, 68–69, *69*
banishment of, 134
complaints about Nur by, 85
as escort to Kashmir, 75
Jahangir kidnapped by, 118–20, 122–32, *126–27*
Jahangir's disputes with, 120–22
Nur's defeat of, 131–35, *133*
Shah Jahan pursued by, 114–15, 117
in Shah Jahan's battle for throne, 137
and Shah Jahan's rebellion, 111

Malik Ambar, 58, *58*
death of, 130
Deccan campaign, 65, 66
resistance to Mughal rule, 84, 103

Malik Masud, 5–6, 8, 11, 13
Malwa, 61
Man Bai, 42
Manucci, Niccolao, 8–10
marriage contracts, 30–31
marriage customs, 92, 93; *See also* weddings
Mathura, 75

INDEX

men
- desirable traits in, 23
- eunuchs, 120
- gatherings of, 51
- within nobles' homes, 20
- and Persian gender divisions, 3

Mihr un Nisa (Sun of Women), xiii; *See also* Nur
- birth of, 2, 8–11, *9*
- in caravan from Persia to India, 8–12
- in caravan through India, 12–14
- daughter Ladli born to, 34–35
- death of Quli, 39
- early life in Lahore for, 13, 14
- education of, 21–23, *22*
- growing up in Agra, 23–26
- growing up in Fatehpur-Sikri, 19–23
- in Jahangir's harem, 40–45
- marriage to Jahangir, 45–47, *46–47*, 47
- marriage to Quli, 27–31, *28–29*, 31–35
- poetry of, 23
- in the Red City, 14–18
- renamed as Nur Mahal, 47
- Salim's/Jahangir's attraction to, 27, 38
- sources on, 10–11

"mirror of happiness," 30, 31
money, given to the needy, 21
Mughal Empire
- under Akbar, *xiv–xv*
- battle for Jahangir's successor in, 137, 140–44
- court culture, 92
- court etiquette, 18
- culture of, 21, 53, 92
- discontent among court members, 109–10
- eunuchs in, 120
- following Shah Jahan's rebellion, 112–13
- Ghiyas's descendants married to emperors in, 97
- gift-giving in, 55
- histories of, 37, 140
- peripatetic (traveling) court, 52–60, *53–55*, 65, 102–6
- powerful women in, 51
- royal hunting in, 62
- successors to emperors in, 93, 109

Mughals (royal family), 2
Muhammad Hadi, 128
Muhammad Sharif, 39
Muhammad Salih Kanbo, 146
Mulla Kami Shirazi, 124, 128, 135
Mumtaz Mahal, 100; *See also* Arjumand

170

INDEX

Muqarrab Khan, 123

music, 14, 35

Mutamad Khan
    battle of 1626 written about by, 128
    and Mahabat's kidnapping of Jahangir, 122, 123, 125

Nadim, 125

Nur (Nur Mahal; Nur Jahan), *xvi*, 60, *149*; *See also* Mihr un Nisa (Sun of Women)
    after Jahangir's death, 146–47
    buildings designed by, 78
    as co-sovereign, 57, 60–61, 65–73, 113
    death of, 148
    defeat of Shah Jahan by, 137
    delayed honeymoon of Jahangir and, 83–92
    fall from power, 145
    garden tomb commissioned by, *104–5*, 105–6
    and Ghiyas's death, 103
    Ghiyas's property given to, 103–4
    gifts to Khurram from, 54–56, *56*, 66–67, *67*
    Heart-Contenting Garden designed by, 142
    historical accounts of, 140, 145–46, 148–49
    hunting by, 61–64, *63*, 75–78, *76*, *77*
    influence of, 48–52, 85
    inn designed by, 78–79, *79*
    and Jahangir's funeral rites, 141–43
    and Jahangir's kidnapping, 119–32, *126–27*
    Jahangir's tomb designed by, 146, 147
    kindness and generosity of, 48, 49
    Ladli's husband chosen by, 91–94
    and Ladli's wedding to Shahryar, 95, 98, 100
    land grants to, 60, 66
    leadership qualities of, 60–61, 149–50
    life and work of, 145–50
    Mahabat defeated by, 131–35, *135*
    Mihr renamed as, 47
    Nur's own tomb designed by, 147
    poetry by, 57, 90
    portrait of, 78–82
    power and authority of, 51–52, 57
    relationship of Jahangir and, 47, 50–51
    royal family group of, 49–50
    and Shah Jahan's battle for the throne, 137, 140–44
    and Shah Jahan's rebellion, 107–17

Nur (Nur Mahal; Nur Jahan) (*continued*)
   during Shah Jahan's reign, 145–46
   and Shahryar's disease, 138
   Shahryar supported by, 93–94, 100–101
   sources on, 10–11
   travels with Jahangir, 52–55, *53–55*, 59
   wedding dresses for poor brides designed by, 48
   worth of commerce and estates owned by, 147
Nurpur (City of Light), 90
Nur's Waterfall, 88, *88*

Orissa, 115

Padshah (sovereign; monarch), 70
Pakhli, 84
Parvez, xiii, 43, *43*
   illness of, 130
   Mahabat's attempted conspiracy with, 121
   and Shah Jahan's rebellion, 115, 117
Pashtu, 60
peripatetic court, 52–60, *53–55*, 65, 102–6

Persia, 2
   culture of, 2–3
   influence in Lahore, 13–14
   Kandahar fort seized by, 107–13
   language of, 34, 35
poetry
   about Nur, 64
   family's love for, 23
   during men's gatherings, 51
   by Nur (Mihr), 23, 57, 90
   Persian, 14
   Persian King of Poets, 90
   by Shirazi, 128, 135
portrait
   of Nur Jahan, 78–82
   of Shahryar, 98
princes; *See also specific princes*
   rebellions by, 109
   symbols of adulthood for, 101
Prophet Muhammad, 113
Punjab, 2–3, 114, 135

Quran, 34, 66

Radha, 75
Rahim, 30
Raja Man Singh, 32
Rajouri, 139
Rajputs, 121, 131
Rama, 25, 26

Ramayana, 25–26

Ramsar, 66

Ravana, 26

red, motif of, 106

Red City, *See* Fatehpur-Sikri

religions

   in Bengal, 34

   Christianity, 3, 10

   Hinduism, 21, 61, 66, 103

   Islam, 3, 8, 16, 24–25, 34, 113, 135

   Judaism, 3

   in Persia, 3

Roe, Thomas, *69*, 69–70

Rose Garden, The (Sadi), 20

Rubaiyat, x

Rumi, 23

Ruqayya Begum, 45

Sadi, 20

Safavids, 108

Sakka, 32

Salim, xiii

   at Akbar's meetings, 17

   as fourth Mughal emperor, 36

   inhumane acts and rebellion against Akbar by, 37–38

   Mihr admired by, 27

   as model for elite boys, 26

   name Jahangir chosen by, 36; *See also* Jahangir

   Quli's distance from, 37–38

   Quli's title from, 34

Salima Begum, 45

Salim Chishti, 16

Saraswati, 34

Shah Abbas, 108

Shahdara, 143, 144

Shah Jahan, 66; *See also* Khurram

   Asaf's support for, 95–96, 110–11, 140

   in battle for the throne, 137, 140–44

   and Khusraw's death, 107

   marriages of, 91–92

   as new emperor, 144–45

   Nur's defeat of, 137

   Nur's history revised by, 140, 146, 148

   Nur's power threatened by, 91–94, 100–101

   rebellion by, 107–17, *116*, 134

   reign of, 145–46

   on second operation in Deccan, 84, 92, 103, 108, 109, 111

   Taj Mahal tribute by, 100

Shahryar, xiii, 43, *43*

   in battle for the throne, 140–44

   chosen as Ladli's husband, 93–94

   execution of, 144

   during Jahangir's kidnapping, 123, 124, 128

INDEX

Shahryar (*continued*)
   Kandahar forces commanded by, 109
   Nur's support for, 93–94, 100–101
   on return following kidnapping, 136
   wedding of Ladli and, 93–100, *96–97*
Shah Shuja, 65, 76, 141, 147
Silk Road, 5
Sind battle, 137
Sita, 25, 26
Srinagar, 84, 89–90
Sulaiman Mountains, 108

Taj Mahal, 100, 106
Tales of the Parrot, 19
taslim, 18, 143
Thousand and One Nights, The, 19–20
Tieffenthaler, Josef, 106
tiger hunting, 75–78, *76, 77*
Toda, 66, 70
trade, 5–6
travel
   from Agra to Bengal, 31–32
   from Agra to Kandahar, 108
   in caravans, 5–14, *6–7*
   to Hardwar, 102–3
   of Jahangir's court, 52–60, *53–55*, 65, 102–6
   to Kashmir, 74–78
   from Lahore to Kabul, 118
Travels in the Mogul Empire (Bernier), 90–91

Vedanta, 61

Wak-Wak Tree, 19–20, 35
weddings, 66
   of Ladli and Shahryar, 93–100, *96–97, 99*
   Mihr and Jahangir, 45–47, *46–47*
   Mihr and Quli, 27–31, *28–29*
   of orphans and poor people, 48
   weighing of the emperor ceremony, 50, 102
women
   with authority and sovereignty, 70–72
   harems for, 41–42; *See also* harems
   within nobles' homes, 20
   in paintings, 81